Screen Design
Strategies for Computer-Assisted
Instruction

Screen Design Strategies for Computer-Assisted Instruction

Jesse M. Heines

DIGITAL PRESS

Printed in U.S.A.

10 9 8 7 6 5 4 3 2

Library of Congress Cataloging in Publication

Heines, Jesse M.
    Screen design strategies for computer-aided instruction.

    Bibliography: p.
    Includes index.
    1. Computer-assisted instruction. 2. Information systems display—Formatting. I. Title.
    LB1028.5.H36 1984   371.3'9445   83-23910
    ISBN 0-932376-28-2

Trademarks
PASS® is a registered trademark of Bell & Howell Co.; Pet® a registered trademark of Commodore Business Machines, Inc.; PLATO® a registered trademark of Control Data Corporation; TICCIT® a registered trademark of Hazeltine Corporation; TRS-80® a registered trademark of Tandy Corporation.

This book is dedicated to
Scott Douglas Heines and Russell Gordon Heines
in the hope that they will always remember
The Little Engine That Could:
if you think you can, you can.

Contents

Preface

This book introduces the major concepts in designing video displays for Computer-Assisted Instruction (CAI). The text does not present a pragmatic "how to" formula for designing video displays, nor does it teach the rudiments of any specific CAI system such as PLATO®[1], TICCIT®[2], or the like. Rather, it attempts to sensitize you to the major variables in the field. The design skills you gain from reading this book will help prepare you to apply your own teaching and curriculum development skills to the creation of effective instructional materials for the computer/video medium.

The design of effective computer screens requires knowledge of the special characteristics of computer-driven screens, an artistic sense of layout and balance, creativity, and sensitivity to the characteristics of the people who will be viewing the screens. The discussion in this book focuses on the special characteristics of computer-driven screens, explores what the computer/video medium can do, and presents the pros and cons of a large number of display techniques. Artistry, creativity, and sensitivity are discussed in relation to the examples, but not exhaustively. I have attempted to provide a set of techniques that you can apply to your courseware when appropriate, rather than presenting rules that are applicable in all situations. You must use your own artistic sense, creativity, and knowledge of your students to adapt these techniques and make them appropriate within your instructional setting.

This is not a book on computer graphics. Although a number of graphic techniques for creating symbols and emphasizing text is presented, the role of graphics in CAI is not explored exhaustively.

---

1. PLATO® is a registered trademark of Control Data Corporation.
2. TICCIT® is a registered trademark of Hazeltine Corporation.

Graphics are certainly an important factor in screen design, but I take the view that they are just one facet of overall screen design and I discuss graphic techniques from this perspective.

I assume that all readers of this text have some familiarity with computers; in short, that they are "computer literate." You should have some idea of what computers are generally designed to do; that is, accept input, process data, and output results. You may already have a feel for what types of operations computers can be easily programmed to perform and what types are more difficult to implement. Knowledge of a computer programming language will be helpful, but more from a conceptual point of view than a technical one. The book contains very few programming examples, and these are presented algorithmically so that they can be understood by anyone who has had minimal exposure to computers.

I also assume that readers have some knowledge of educational technology, the "soft" science of communicating information from one person to another in such a way that the receiver retains that information for some length of time. The basic tenets of the technology to which I am referring are:

- the stating of instructional outcomes in measurable terms,
- the use of task analysis to determine what has to be taught to achieve those outcomes,
- the systematic development and evaluation of instructional materials,
- the measurement of instructional outcomes through testing, and
- the revision of instructional materials based on empirical data on their usage.

These principles and their applications are discussed in virtually all introductory texts on educational psychology and educational technology.

This book is designed as a basic text. Each chapter focuses on one aspect of screen design and contains activities designed to reinforce the concepts introduced. Completion of the exercises usually requires access to an interactive computer system and the writing of short computer programs, and some exercises require access to systems with specific capabilities. It is unlikely that you will be able to complete all of the exercises on any single system, but you should be able to complete some of them on any system. The glossary at the end of the book clarifies computer terms and serves as a reference. Most of the terms that are italicized when first introduced are included in the glossary.

You should not try to follow all of the guidelines presented in this book. These guidelines reflect my own experience and style, and some may not be suitable for your student population. As you study this book, try to look at as many CAI programs as you possibly can. Time spent viewing others' work will provide you with invaluable exposure to additional screen design techniques and a fuller understanding of the capabilities of the computer/video medium.

It is my hope that this book will excite you about the potential of the computer/video medium to achieve maximum effectiveness from CAI materials, and help you to design visual displays that are instructionally sound, visually stimulating, and comfortable for students to use.

J.M.H.

Acknowledgments

A number of people have worked with me during development of the ideas in this book, exchanged ideas with me on screen design, and critiqued courseware I have produced. Some of these colleagues are credited with footnotes in the text where direct contributions can be identified. Others had a more pervasive influence, and I thank them for providing insight and clarification to my ideas.

The three people who have had the most sustained influence on my design work in the past few years have been Alfred Bork, Roger Bowker, and Michael Zimmerman. Colleagues who contributed individual design techniques and some special "gems" include Paul Blenkhorn, John Bowers, Peter Dean, Michelle Fineblum, George Gropper, Sue Kilburn, Richard Kirschbaum, Wendy Mackay, Pete McVay, and Ken Moreau.

I wish to thank Gordon Constable for printing the photographs of screen displays shown throughout this book, and the Academic Computing Service of The British Open University for allowing me to use their equipment to prepare both the manuscript and the sample displays.

On the personal side, I wish to thank Evelyn and Jim, two very special friends who provided the encouragement needed to scale the peaks and bridge the valleys. Finally, I thank my mother, Dorothy Heines, for her painstaking review of this manuscript and for teaching me that the pursuit of excellence begins with attention to detail.

Jesse M. Heines
Chelmsford, Mass., U.S.A.
Newport Pagnell, Bucks, England

·1·

The Computer/Video Medium

The days of the hard copy terminal are over. Paper is out, video is in. Compare, for example, the visual quality of the graph printed by a teletypewriter shown in Figure 1-1 against the quality of the video display shown in Figure 1-2. On large time-sharing systems, television-like terminals are quickly replacing their typewriter-like counterparts. More importantly, the microcomputers that are on their way to becoming standard equipment in today's classrooms are virtually all designed to take advantage of the special characteristics of computer-driven displays. It is still possible, of course, to do effective computer-assisted instruction (CAI) on teletypewriters and similar devices that print on paper at slow speeds, but their days as viable instructional media are numbered.

Some students do not feel comfortable with any course unless they receive or produce something on paper that they can take away. This reaction is a carry-over from traditional study methods, but it can be very strong. In most cases, the need for paper can be satisfied by giving students copies of summary displays, a student guide, or a printed diploma.

Today's true CAI medium should be thought of as a combination of a computer and a video display. It is a *computer/video* medium. While the visual capabilities of this medium fall short of those achieved by standard television, except in the most sophisticated and expensive systems, using this medium merely as a frame for displaying pages of text makes little use of its visual power and strangles its ability to enhance instruction (compare Figures 1-3 and 1-4).

1

```
      0...OXYGEN-SCALE....5...OXYGEN-SCALE...10...OXYGEN-SCALE...15
      0..WASTE.10..SCALE.20..WASTE.30..SCALE.40..WASTE.50..SCALE.60
DAY   I---------I---------I---------I---------I---------I---------I
 0    I W                                      O
 1    I       W                                O
 2    I            W                        O
 3    I               W           O
 4    I                         WO
 5    I                         O   W
 6    I                       O        W
 7    I                     O            W
 8    I                   O              W
 9    I                   O                 W
10    I                   O                 W
11    I                  O                    W
12    I                  O                      W
13    I                  O                      W
14    I                  O                        W
15    I                  O                        W
16    I                  O                        W
17    I                  O                        W
18    I                  O                        W
```

FIGURE 1-1.   *A Graph Printed by a Teletypewriter.* (*After Braun et al., 1971.*)

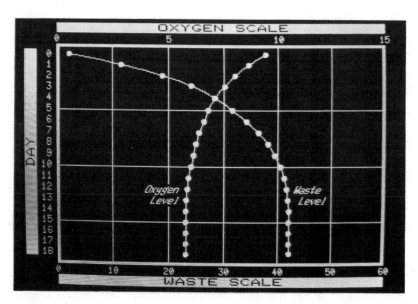

FIGURE 1-2.   *A Graph Printed on a Video Screen.*

This chapter discusses the overall characteristics of the computer/video medium that impact design of instructional materials. It be-

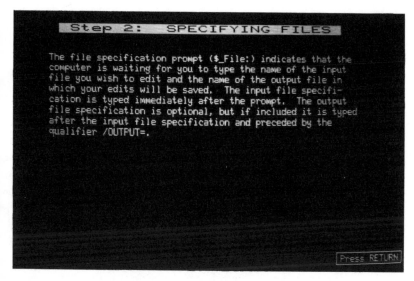

FIGURE 1-3. *A Visual Display Using Text Only.*

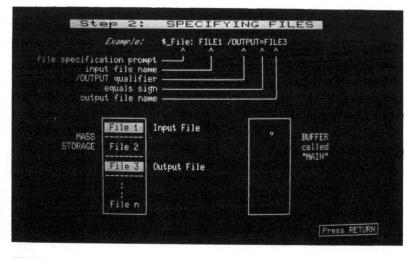

FIGURE 1-4. *A Visual Display Using Text and Graphics.*

gins by highlighting the design differences between a video display and a printed page. It defines resolution, describes how it relates to computer/video systems, and explains the qualities of systems with different levels of resolution. The chapter concludes by examining different role models for video screen design and exploring their pros and cons.

The Display vs. The Page

A number of important differences distinguish the video display from the printed page. For example, information may be written anywhere on a computer screen at any time. It need not start at the upper left-hand corner and proceed in typewriter-like fashion to the bottom right. This characteristic allows video displays to be dynamic: one part of the screen can be erased and rewritten while another part remains unchanged.

Blank space on computer screens is "free" (Bork, 1982). Unlike paper-based media, the presence of large amounts of blank space does not increase printing and reproduction costs. Information that should be logically separated for either conceptual or aesthetic reasons can easily be presented on two different displays, because it is no more expensive to use two displays than it is to use one.   .

The computer/video medium has a dimension of time. Information can be displayed on the screen slowly or quickly, pausing at selected points to provide special emphasis (Bork, 1982). The time dimension also allows most computer/video media to perform limited animation sequences. This technique has been shown to be extremely useful for illustrating certain types of concepts, as well as highly powerful for capturing and holding student interest in educational games.

While the computer/video medium may at first appear to offer only positive influences on computerized instruction, it does have several drawbacks when compared closely with its hard copy predecessor. For example, it is often difficult for students to back up and review material presented on a video screen. If hard copy is not available, students cannot take the material away to study at home. In addition, it can be difficult for teachers to decipher the thinking processes of students who are having trouble if they cannot recall specific visual displays and retrace those students' steps.

The excitement of the computer/video medium must therefore be tempered with a realization of its implications. The medium's many unique characteristics discussed in the chapters that follow must be used thoughtfully if they are to be effective. At its worst, the computer/video medium can seriously confuse students with a barrage of disjointed visual effects. Indiscriminate use of video features such as color and non-standard writing can hinder rather than enhance communication between the computer and the student. At its best, however, the computer/video medium offers great promise for enhancing communication between the students and computers.

Picture Resolution

The fundamental design parameter for any visual medium is the *resolution* with which pictures can be displayed. Pictures with coarse resolution are grainy and exhibit sharp breaks from one picture element to the next. Pictures with fine resolution are smooth, and each picture element appears to blend into the adjoining elements. The resolution exhibited by any particular system depends on the type of video display system being used and the computer's internal representation of the picture.

Types of Video Display Systems

The basic picture element of virtually all computer screens is a dot of light. Such dots are often called *pixels*, an abbreviation for "picture element," and represent the smallest possible entity that can be displayed on the screen. Most computer screens commonly used for CAI are made up of thousands of pixels, arranged in a series of rows and columns. Video displays of this type are referred to as *raster scan systems*. The term "raster" refers to the array of pixels, and "scan" refers to the sequential manner in which the television's electron beam moves across each row of pixels in turn, lighting only those pixels appropriate to the image or message to be displayed. For a raster scan system to draw a vertical line, it must begin at the upper left-hand corner of the screen, scan across the first row and light the appropriate pixel, finish scanning that row and move to the beginning of the next, scan over and light the appropriate pixel on that row, and so on.

Another type of video display is the *stroke vector system*. Here the electron beam can be positioned at any point and then moved directly to any other point without having to scan the screen in rows. For a stroke vector system to draw a vertical line, it simply positions the electron beam at the starting point and moves directly up or down to the end point. While stroke vector systems sound much simpler conceptually, they are much more expensive to build. For this reason, very few such systems are now used for CAI, although the work of Alfred Bork at the University of California at Irvine represents a notable exception (see Bork, 1981). With the exception of one or two clearly identified comments about stroke vector systems, the displays referred to from here on are all raster scan systems.

Picture Representation in Dot Matrices

The array of pixels that make up the display area of a raster scan system is commonly referred to as a *dot matrix*. The resolution of any particular dot matrix is determined by the distance between dots. If one system represents pictures in a dot matrix with 511 rows of 767 columns while another system employs a matrix with 159 rows of 279 columns, the former is said to have "higher" or "greater" or "finer" resolution than the latter (assuming the overall screen sizes are the same).

Picture resolution is a function of both the video monitor (television) on which the picture is being viewed and the computer that is driving it. Some video monitors have inherently higher resolution than others. For example, American standard televisions have 525 rows of dots, while European standard televisions have 625 rows. For applications such as filmmaking that demand extremely high-quality computer graphics, televisions are available with 1000 rows of dots. The greater the number of dots, the greater the *potential* picture resolution. The ultimate resolution of any computer/video system is determined by the physical potential of the screen and the size of the dot matrix that the computer uses to represent that screen. That is, two computer systems might employ the same television as an output device, but one might represent the screen internally with a 128 by 256 dot matrix while the other uses a 256 by 512 dot matrix. In this case, the latter system will have greater resolution than the former.

Pictures on dot matrix screens are drawn by determining the locations of the points in the picture and then "turning on" those dots that correspond to desired points. Compare the photograph in Figure 1-5 with the corresponding line drawing created within the dot matrix of a computer screen shown in Figure 1-6, and note the apparent roughness of the computer picture. This roughness is a direct consequence of the lower resolution of the computer screen.

Some simple figures, like boxes and horizontal lines, can be presented precisely on computer screens if the points in the figure corre-

FIGURE 1-5. *Photo Used for Creation of Figure 1-6.*

FIGURE 1-6. *Outline of Photograph in Figure 1-5 Drawn Within a Dot Matrix.*

pond exactly to dots in the matrix. More complex figures, such as those involving curves, must usually be approximated. No matter how fine the resolution, all dot matrix displays exhibit discontinuities caused

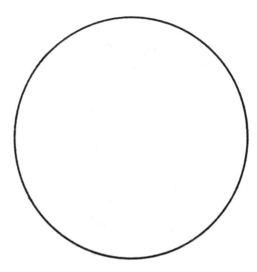

FIGURE 1-7. *A Printed Circle. Note that the edges are perfectly smooth.*

FIGURE 1-8. *A Circle Drawn Within a Dot Matrix. Note the discontinuities in the edges caused by* staircasing.

by these approximations. Such discontinuities are referred to as *stair-casing*, because line segments and curves sometimes resemble staircases rather than smooth slopes (compare Figures 1-7 and 1-8). The degree of staircasing depends on the resolution of the screen, the nature of the figure being drawn, and the specific algorithm used by the computer to determine which points to turn on. Thus, as shown in Figure 1-9, lines drawn at different angles exhibit different degrees of staircasing. By drawing a figure in relation to the characteristics of the dot matrix, you can sometimes control the degree of staircasing.

FIGURE 1-9.   *Lines Exhibiting Various Degrees of Staircasing.*

Staircasing is sometimes called *aliasing* in more technical graphics literature. The main advantage of stroke vector systems is that they do not exhibit staircasing. There are also a number of *anti-aliasing* techniques that can be used to downplay staircasing on raster scan systems, even though it can never be totally eliminated. Such techniques require very expensive equipment and are therefore beyond the scope of systems commonly used for CAI.

Bit Maps

Systems that allow you to address each individual dot on the screen and turn them on and off independently actually contain a special section of memory that "maps" the screen. This map consists of a series of "bits" for each dot indicating whether that dot is on or off, what color it is, etc. This internal representation is called the screen's *bit map*, and systems that employ this technique are said to have *bit-mapped screens*. The hardware and software techniques for implementing bit-mapped screens are not new, but they are limited by the size of the computer's memory. As the cost of memory continues to decline, bit-mapped screens are becoming increasingly popular, even on inexpensive systems.

Character Cells

Even though virtually all systems used for large-scale CAI today make use of bit-mapped screens, a number of viable systems do exist that do not allow you to really address each individual dot. (This limitation may be caused by either the hardware or the software, but it is a firm limitation nonetheless.) These limited systems usually restrict addressing to the level of *character cells,* the small array of dots that make up a single character. Thus, a screen might consist of 720 dots horizontally and 240 dots vertically, but these might only be addressable in character cells of 9 by 10 dots (horizontal by vertical, see Figure 1-10). Such an arrangement applies to many standard industrial screens that have 24 rows of 80 characters ($80 \times 9 = 720$, and $24 \times 10 = 240$).

A set of dot patterns that defines meaningful characters is referred to as a *character set.* For example, most systems have a character set containing the letters of the alphabet, the numerals, and a set of punctuation marks. Many systems that are restricted to character cell level addressing also have an auxiliary *graphics character set* with special dot patterns for drawing simple figures. Figure 1-11 shows part of a graphics character set that is particularly well-suited for drawing rectangles.

Before an auxiliary character set can be used, you must issue a command that puts the system into *graphics mode.* When the system is functioning in graphics mode, information sent to the screen is interpreted as either graphics commands or special characters rather than letters to be displayed. For example, putting a video system into graphics mode and printing the lowercase letters shown in Figure 1-11 can

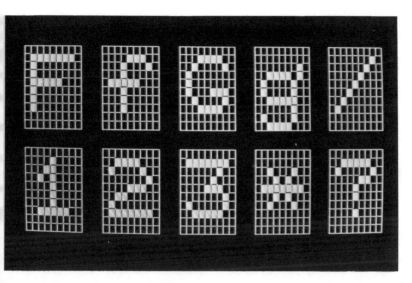

FIGURE 1-10. *9 by 10 Character Cells.*

FIGURE 1-11. *Part of a Graphics Character Set.*

cause the corresponding graphics characters to be displayed. These graphics characters can be combined in a variety of ways to draw simple figures. For example, Figure 1-12 shows a rectangle drawn using the graphics character set of Figure 1-11 and identifies the letters printed in

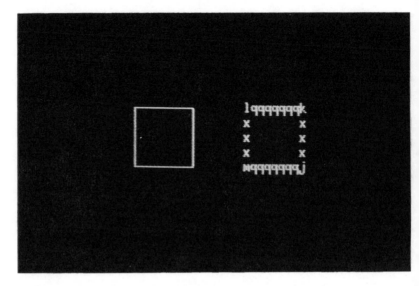

FIGURE 1-12.   *A Rectangle Drawn Using the Graphics Character Set in Figure 1-11.*

graphics mode to generate the picture. As shown in Figures 1-13 and 1-14, you can actually draw quite nice figures with these character sets, as long as those figures are made up of simple horizontal and vertical lines.

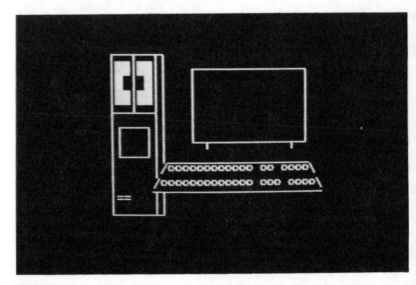

FIGURE 1-13.   *A Figure Drawn Using the Graphics Character Set in Figure 1-11.*

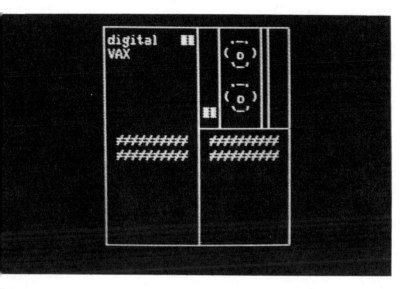

IGURE 1-14. *A Figure Drawn Using the Graphics Character Set in Figure*
-11.

.ole Models for Screen Design

he computer/video medium, while unique in some respects, is not com-
letely new. Certainly the screen designer can learn important concepts
nd borrow techniques from associated media, particularly graphic art,
lm, and television.

;raphic Art

erhaps the clearest relation exists between video screen design and
raphic art. While it is often difficult to display photographic images on
omputer screens, most systems make it quite straightforward to display
raphic entities such as lines, boxes, circles, blocks, and various text
tyles.

There are two reasons, however, why graphic art is not a perfect
ole model for computer screens. First, the resolution of most graphic
iedia (posters, magazines, and even newspapers) is far finer than that
f the video displays commonly used for CAI. Second, graphic art is
enerally static, while computer screens have a number of dynamic
roperties.

Television and Film

Images on computer screens can be built up slowly or quickly, picture
can be overlaid and changed, and entities can be made to move abou
on the screen in an animated fashion. These techniques resemble fea
tures of television and film, but these media are not perfect role model
either, for two main reasons. First, the ability of television and film t
display photographic images far exceeds that of most computer/vide
systems, while television's ability to display text is usually far inferio
Second, computer screens are usually viewed from only half a meter o
less, while television and film are generally viewed from a distance of a
least two meters.

Informational Television

Perhaps the best role model, then, is a combination of graphic art an
what might be called *informational television,* the type of broadcastin
commonly found in news programs, documentaries, sporting events
children's educational programs, and even commercials. Such broad
casts make extensive use of graphics and often overlay text onto othe
visual images. In addition, these broadcasts *never* display a full scree
of text they intend the viewer to read.

   Informational television and CAI differ significantly, of course, be
cause virtually all television programs have an audio component whil
most CAI programs do not. It is clear, however, that the amount o
data carried in informational television's visual component is far greate
than that carried in its audio component. (To prove this to yourself, tr
Activity 5 at the end of this chapter.) Thus, the CAI screen designe
should employ both graphics and textual messages to communicate wit
the student.

Chapter Summary

The video displays used on most CAI systems today possess characte
istics significantly different from the teletypewriters and other hard cop
terminals that preceded them. These differences have a number of im
plications for CAI and require the screen designer to be sensitive to
host of capabilities unique to the computer/video medium.

The fundamental design parameter for any visual medium is its resolution. Computer/video systems exhibit varying degrees of resolution depending upon the types of televisions they use for output and the internal size of the bit map they use to represent the screen. Even though virtually all video displays used for CAI are made up of dots, some systems do not actually allow you to address each individual dot and turn them on and off independently. Many systems with this limited functionality provide graphics character sets as a substitute method for drawing pictures.

The best role model for the computer/video medium is informational television such as one finds in news broadcasts. This model combines graphic art with text and moving images to yield dynamic displays that are literally packed with information. While screen design techniques can be adapted from static graphic art and other related media, the combination of computer and video display is sufficiently unique to warrant special study.

Issues and Activities

1. Experiment with any computer display to which you have access to determine its capabilities. Can you write anywhere on the screen at any time? Can you control the rate at which text is displayed? Can you easily draw lines and boxes and circles on the screen?

2. Determine the type of addressing that your system supports. Is your system bit-mapped or does it support only character cell level addressing?

3. If your system supports only character cell level addressing, does it support an alternate graphics character set? If so, what types of figures can you draw by combining the shapes in that character set?

4. Use the graphics character set shown in Figure 1-11 plus the characters "/" and "\" to draw a picture of a house. Indicate the letters you would print in graphics mode to generate the picture.

5. Watch a documentary or children's program with the sound turned off for a few minutes and see how much you can follow. Then listen to the program's audio track without the picture for the same length of time. Which component, the audio or the video, was easier to follow on its own? Which one carried more information?

6. View some CAI programs that were written specifically for a video display. Can you see any conscious designs in the screen layouts?

Are the visual images unrelated or do they exhibit some continuity from one lesson to the next? How might you improve on the authors' designs?

7. Would your students feel more comfortable with CAI if some paper-based materials were available? If so, how might you satisfy this need while maintaining the video screen as your major communication medium? Can you generate hard copy directly from screen displays on your system?

8. Hardware availability continues to be a major roadblock to CAI even though the increasing use of low-cost microcomputers has eased the situation. Could you use CAI at all if you had only one system for your entire class? How about if you had 2, or 4, or 8? How many systems would you need to make CAI a viable instructional adjunct in your classroom?

9. Compare the resolution on a number of different computer/video systems. What factors determine the resolution of each? Which are limited by their hardware, and which by their software?

10. Draw a number of simple figures such as circles and triangles and diagonal lines on your computer/video system. How severe is the staircasing? What can you do to reduce staircasing on your system?

·2·

Functional Areas

Erasing a video display initializes it to a blank screen. Information can then be displayed anywhere on the screen in virtually any order and at a number of speeds. Such freedom, however, requires control so that students are not inundated by flashy techniques that generate visual confusion and do little to enhance communication.

One of the simplest techniques for organizing CAI displays is to divide the screen into a number of specific *functional areas* and use these in a consistent manner throughout the course. For example, the top part of the screen could be reserved for diagrams and the bottom part for explanation of those diagrams. Functional areas need not be completely static throughout an entire course; they might shrink and grow as the ratio of graphics to textual information changes. But consistent use of general screen areas for certain types of information can help students maintain their orientation and minimize the effort needed to decipher what the program is asking them to do. In addition, consistent use of functional areas can ease the transition from one instructional unit to the next, allowing students to concentrate on the subject matter rather than on the mechanics of taking a computerized course.

This chapter introduces the concept of functional areas and explains why they are important factors in screen design. It lists standard screen components, states the purpose of each, and relates them to functional area concepts. The chapter examines the considerations involved in choosing which areas of the screen to use for specific functions. It concludes by discussing a number of different techniques for clearing functional areas and their instructional implications.

17

Standard Screen Components

CAI displays should contain a number of standard components, whether the instructional sequence involves drill and practice, simulation, problem solving, or simply presentation of new information. Such components include:

- orientation information,
- directions,
- student responses,
- error messages, and
- student options.

These five components are discussed in the following pages.

Orientation Information

Two of the most common questions students ask themselves as they work through any instructional material are, "How much have I done?" and "How much more do I have to do?" With paper-based media such as books, students can easily see at a glance how many pages they have read and how many remain to the end of the book or chapter. Even with audiovisual media, students can usually figure out where they are by keeping track of the running time (assuming the program is linear).

Branching CAI materials present a much more complex orientation problem. Not only is it virtually impossible for students to figure out answers to the two questions quoted above, but they can completely lose their awareness of where they are if the program branches them, for example, to a remedial sequence which is conceptually somewhat removed from the current context. That is, students doing poorly on a simulation exercise might be branched to a more elementary drill session on a specific subskill required for the simulation. Without orientation data, this branch can be somewhat disconcerting as these students wonder if they will ever get back to the simulation.

The *orientation information* needed can usually be supplied very simply by putting the current module name and lesson name at the top of the screen. This orientation technique can be thought of as running heads like the titles and subtitles that often appear on each page of a book. The module and lesson names are most often displayed in a somewhat subdued manner if possible. The subdued effect might be achieved by using a small text size, a quiet color, or *reverse video* (dark letters on a white background, sometimes referred to as *inverse video*). The important point is to set the orientation information off from other display entities so it is there if students need it, but its presence does not interfere with the overall presentation of the subject matter being discussed (see Figure 2-1).

Orientation information can also play an important role during program *debugging*, because it helps pinpoint where a program error occurred. If an error is reported together with its module and lesson name, it will be much easier for instructors to find, isolate, and correct the error than if students simply report that the program "bombed out."

Student Directions and Responses

The next two major components of CAI displays are the *directions* telling students what they are expected to do and the *responses* that the students type. These two components are considered together because they are often adjacent or share the same functional area. Some displays, particularly certain types of simulations, might not have directions if students are expected to run the simulation without being

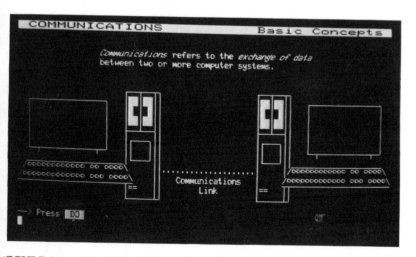

FIGURE 2-1. *Orientation Information in Reverse Video at the Top of a Screen.*

prompted. Most displays, however, provide information about what students should do next, even if they are simply to press the RETURN key. In addition, displays that require students to type responses usually *echo* those responses by displaying them on the screen as they are typed. Many CAI programs that expect typed responses wait for students to press a key such as RETURN before evaluating those responses and taking the appropriate action.

Both of these compon nts are best reserved for a specific functional area. That way, studer s always know where to look for directions, even if the screen is changing constantly (as it often does in sophisticated simulations), and where to expect their typed responses to appear. The fact that directions might take up considerably more space on one screen than on another does not cause a serious problem. As stated earlier, functional areas can grow and shrink to accommodate such variations, but a specific function should always appear in the same general area on the screen. If this is not possible, strong visual clues should be used to draw students' attention to these areas as they move about. (The use of visual indicators and symbols to provide these clues is discussed in Chapter 3.)

Error Messages

The fourth screen component is *error messages* and is one of the most important components to reserve for a specific functional area. The error messages referred to here are not feedback that explains incorrect responses. Rather, they are messages printed in response to inappropriate student entries that the computer cannot accept as answers. For example, suppose the computer presents a true/false question with a correct answer of "true." If the student enters "false," the program might provide feedback as to why that answer is incorrect. But if the student enters "no," the program should print an error message stating that the only acceptable answers at this point are "true" and "false."

One of the most popular techniques for informing students that they have made an error is to ring the terminal's bell and print a message explaining the error.[1] This can be a very effective method because

---

1. "Ringing a terminal's bell" is the action that occurs when ASCII character number 7 is sent to the terminal. In BASIC, this is done by executing the statement PRINT CHR$(7), while the equivalent statement in PASCAL is WRITE (CHR(7)). The reference to this action as ringing a bell is purely historical, as most of today's terminals have electric buzzers or beepers instead of bells.

the bell immediately catches students' attention. Once this audio signal is heard, students will probably look at the screen to see what happened. If the screen is complex, it might be difficult to figure out exactly what went wrong. But if error messages always appear at the same point on the screen, students will know just where to look to understand the problem.

The construction of error messages is an art in itself. These messages ought to be meaningful, but they should also be as short as possible. If a student makes the same error a number of times, long error messages can be very annoying. One technique that has been used successfully in a number of systems is to provide two *levels* of error messages. When an error is made, the first level is displayed. This message is usually limited to a few key words, requiring no more than a single line on the screen. The student can then take one of two actions: either re-enter his or her response or type a special character for more detailed explanation of the error. Some systems use a specially designated HELP key to provide access to the second level, while others simply direct students to type a question mark. In either case, display of the resultant error information in a reserved functional area helps maintain student orientation and makes it easier to refresh the screen when the program returns to the learning task.

Student Options

Many CAI systems provide a number of *options* that students can exercise instead of entering responses to questions. For example, students might be able to exit the program, request help, use the computer as a calculator, enter a comment for their instructor, view a summary of the material being presented, go back and review a specific section, etc. (see Figure 2-2). Systems designed specifically for CAI, like PLATO and TICCIT, usually have special keys that students can press at any time to choose these options (PLATO's option keys are shown in Figure 2-3). Other more general systems can still provide these options either through programmable function keys or codes that students can enter instead of answers.

One novel way of providing student options when special function keys are not available is to display them as a *menu* in a reserved func-

---

2. The techniques described here were adapted for CAI by Michael Zimmerman.

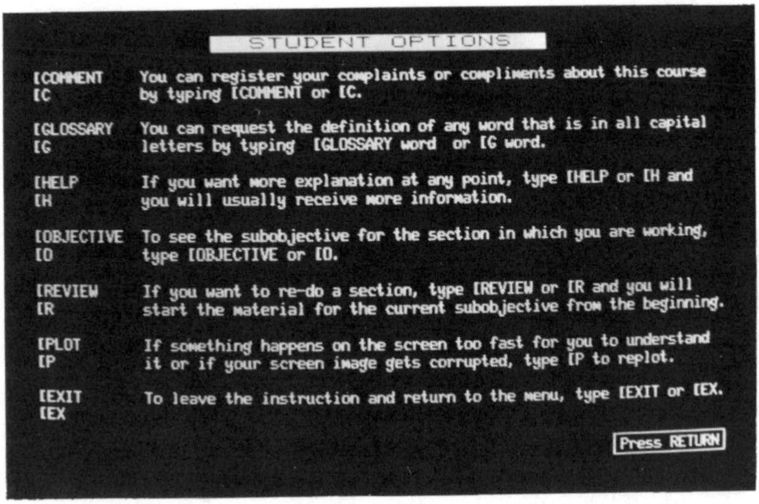

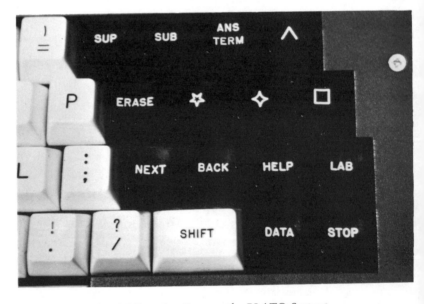

FIGURE 2-2. *Typical Student Options.*

FIGURE 2-3. *Special Function Keys on the PLATO System.*

tional area.[2] (See Figure 2-4; menus and their usage are discussed in detail in Chapter 4.) This technique keeps the options in mind and avoids forcing students to memorize codes for selecting them. The options menu

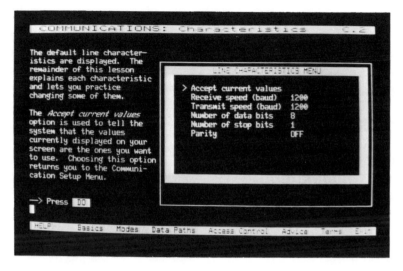

FIGURE 2-4. *A Screen Containing All Recommended Functional Areas.*

itself need not be active at all times. Rather, students might press a HELP key to activate the options menu. This approach was used for the menu shown in Figure 2-4. Pressing the HELP key causes the word HELP preceding the menu to change to CHOOSE, and students can then select an option. As before, the help menu always appears in the same general screen area, so it is easy for students to find and identify.

Choosing Functional Areas

Once you decide what functional areas you will have on your screen, you must choose the shape and general location for each area. For example, you might decide that you will put all orientation information at the top of the screen and reserve the last line on the screen for error messages. These decisions are relatively easy. Choosing functional areas for other screen components, however, can be a bit more difficult. Three important factors in making these choices are:

- area shapes,
- area locations, and
- area boundaries.

Area Shapes

The easiest functional area to work with is the block, a rectangular area that covers some portion of the screen. Blocks may be short and wide or long and narrow. Since the screen itself is a block, it is usually quite easy to find reasonably sized blocks that fit comfortably. Text fits nicely into blocks, as do most figures. The block also has another advantage: many systems have special commands for erasing them quickly and easily.

The screen shown in Figure 2-4 has six functional areas, all in the shape of blocks. The top line is a functional area all by itself and contains the orientation information. This information includes the module title, "COMMUNICATIONS," followed by the lesson title, "Characteristics." The symbols "C.2" at the right indicate that this is the second lesson in Module C (for "Communications"). The bottom line is another functional area, and it contains the options menu discussed previously. Note how these functional areas frame the display and how reverse video is used to distinguish them clearly from the lesson text.

The third functional area on this screen is the simulated menu at the right of the screen. The lesson in this instance teaches the meaning of each option on the menu. Therefore, a simulated menu is displayed and each option is indicated with a right angle bracket (>) as it is explained. All simulated menus in the course appear in this format, providing a high degree of continuity as the context changes from lesson to lesson.

The explanatory text forms the fourth functional area. It always begins at the extreme left of the fourth line on the screen and maintains a constant width, but the length of the area increases or decreases as the amount of text varies. (The various formats in which text can be displayed are discussed in Chapter 5.) This functional area is followed by the directions, which appear one or two lines below the end of the text block and are preceded by the symbol "→" to catch the student's attention. (The use of such symbols is discussed in more detail in Chapter 3.) The sixth and final functional area on this screen comprises the two lines just above the options menu. This area is reserved for error messages (none of which are displayed in Figure 2-4).

Note the position of the *cursor*, the small, solid rectangle near the bottom left of the screen. The cursor indicates where the next character typed by the student will be displayed. (The location of student responses might be considered a functional area on its own. In this case, an area is not needed because students simply press a single key.) The cursor is an important visual factor because it usually attracts the student's eye by flashing. It should be placed thoughtfully to enhance or downplay its draw as the instruction requires. The cursor in Figure 2-4 is positioned to draw students' attention to the direction, "Press DO." As explained a little later, the cursor's location must also be considered when using certain graphics functions.

The use of blocks for these functional areas keeps the screen organized and clear, although perhaps the screen as a whole contains more textual information than is aesthetically pleasing. The explanatory text block at the left of the screen is particularly easy to erase and update, an important feature for this type of instruction.

An earlier design for this screen had the text wrapping around the simulated menu as shown in Figure 2-5. This design was poor for three main reasons. First, there was too much text on the screen. Second, the text lines above and below the simulated menu were too long, making them difficult to read. Third, erasing the text was a complicated process from a visual as well as a programming point of view. The cursor jumped all over the screen as the old text was erased, creating a somewhat disorienting visual effect. This earlier design was therefore abandoned, even though the area available for explanatory text was greater in this design than in the one ultimately adopted.

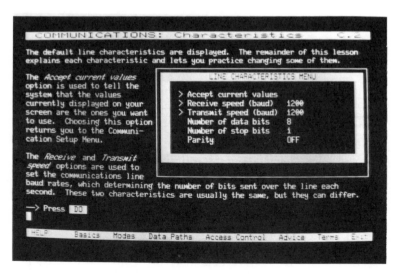

FIGURE 2-5.   A **Poor** *Layout for a Text Area. The text should not wrap around the menu.*

Another screen from the same course is shown in Figure 2-6. Here the lesson objective has changed and a simulated menu is not called for. However, the orientation, options menu, and error message functional areas remain the same. The continuity gained from such design consistency makes it easier for students to concentrate on the subject matter, because it reduces the amount of effort needed to understand the mechanics of the course.

The block shape is usually the only logical choice for a functional area on screens with character cell level addressing although there are, of course, some special situations which call for other shapes. Some figures might fit more logically into circles or triangles than into blocks, but these shapes are difficult to represent on screens with only character cell level addressing. Non-block shapes can be used more easily on bitmapped screens because these screens allow finer control of where characters and pictures will be displayed. You must be careful, however, not to be "taken in" by the capabilities of pixel level addressing to create overly complex screen formats. Such formats can confuse students as easily as they can assist them. CAI authors sometimes devise what they perceive to be "clever" screen formats only to find that the reasons for doing so are generally opaque to students and impair their abilities to focus on the subject matter. Complex formats, whether on character

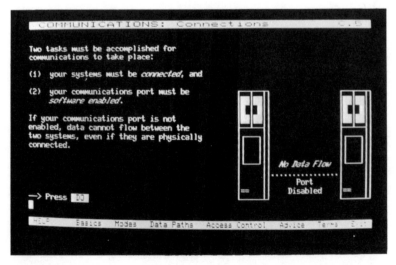

FIGURE 2-6. *Consistent Placement of Functional Areas Even Though the Lesson Objective Has Changed. Compare with Figure 2-4.*

cell or bit-mapped systems, should therefore be used only when truly needed or for special effects.

Area Locations

Screen components such as orientation information and student options are most commonly located at either the top or the bottom of the screen. They might, of course, also be placed in the side margins, but this design has certain side effects when other functional areas are cleared.

For example, suppose that you design a screen with the six functional areas shown in Figure 2-7. A lesson might begin by writing something into each of the first five functional areas (all but the error message area). When the student presses RETURN, you wish to totally rewrite the text area. Most standard CAI systems do not have an "erase block" *primitive.* That is, there is no fast, *simple* way for the hardware or software to erase an arbitrary block area. You might have to overwrite the entire area with "space" characters to erase the block, and this could be a rather slow process. (A faster method for performing block erases that can be implemented on some bit-mapped systems is described later.)

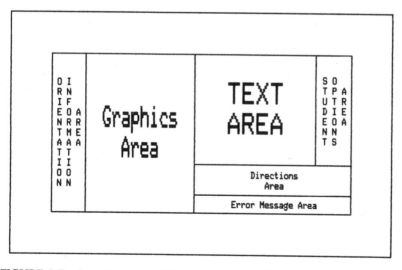

FIGURE 2-7.   Poor *Location of Functional Areas. The text and graphics areas would be difficult to erase with standard screen primitives.*

Most systems do, however, have fast "erase line" primitives, often in the form of "erase from cursor to beginning of line" and/or "erase from cursor to end of line." Unfortunately, the design in Figure 2-7 precludes use of these primitives, because no matter where the cursor is placed in the text area, erasing to the beginning or end of the line will delete part of other areas as well. So this functional area layout is more troublesome than the one in Figure 2-4, where the text area can be erased by using a sequence of "erase to beginning of line" primitives with the cursor positioned just to the left of the simulated menu.

Another reason for locating functional areas horizontally rather than vertically deals with *scrolling*. In most CAI systems, trying to move the cursor down one line when it is already on the last line of the screen causes the entire screen to move upwards one line to create a blank line at the bottom of the screen. This action is often the result of terminating a line of text with a carriage return/line feed pair, which moves the cursor to the beginning of the next line. The line feed character initiates scrolling (see Figure 2-8). Anything that was on the top line of the screen before it scrolled disappears and cannot be retrieved. (It is said to "scroll off" the screen.) Scrolling can be very useful on low-speed displays because it eliminates the need to erase a functional area before rewriting it. That is, if you rewrite the area using scrolling, the old text will be erased automatically when it disappears off the top of the screen.

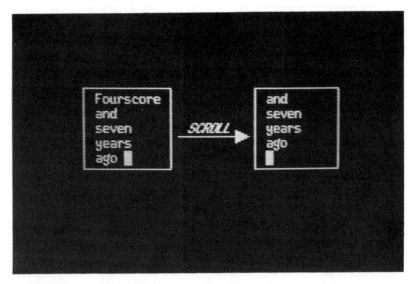

FIGURE 2-8. *Demonstration of Scrolling.*

While some CAI systems (most notably PLATO) do not scroll at all and others scroll only the entire screen, more sophisticated systems allow screen designers to define restricted *scrolling regions*. These regions are usually defined by indicating to the system the top and bottom lines to scroll. In Figure 2-9, for example, the scrolling region is lines 2–4 inclusive. When a line feed is printed on the last line of the scrolling region, only the lines within the scrolling region move up. Lines outside the scrolling region are not affected.

The use of scrolling regions is often referred to as *split screen scrolling,* and' most systems with this capability allow the screen to be split only along full horizontal lines. That is, if the scrolling region is defined as lines 4–6, *everything* on these lines will be scrolled. Thus, this technique would *not* be usable with the functional area designs in either Figure 2-4 or Figure 2-7. It would, however, be usable with the design in Figure 2-1. The explanatory text area at the top of that screen could be scrolled without affecting any other functional area.

Vertical scrolling is by far the most common type of scrolling on CAI terminals. Some systems, however, also allow horizontal scrolling, or *creeping,* as it is called in television jargon. A common example of creeping is the display of a moving line of text along the bottom of a television screen to broadcast a news bulletin without interrupting the program currently being aired. Note that creeping is easier than vertical

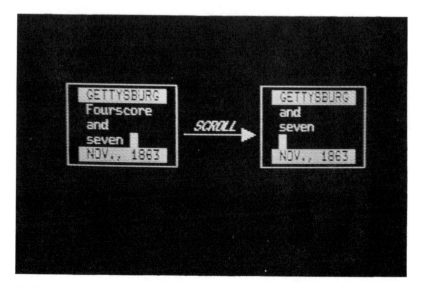

FIGURE 2-9. *Demonstration of Scrolling Regions (Split Screen Scrolling).*

scrolling to simulate via software, particularly if lines are kept short. It is therefore a viable technique even on systems that do not support it as a primitive.

Area Boundaries

The major reasons for using functional areas are clarity, consistency, and continuity. But do not become a fanatic about reserving screen areas if it makes sense to extend a functional area temporarily beyond its normal bounds, even if that extension makes it overlap with another area. Each reserved area takes up space on the screen, and this space can sometimes be at a premium. Do not be afraid to omit or overwrite a functional area temporarily if it intrudes on the overall lesson design. Such omissions will hardly be noticed if the lesson as a whole follows a clear and consistent design.

Interestingly enough, area boundaries can sometimes be put to excellent use when emphasis is desired. For example, look at the effects created in Figure 2-10. The text is the same size in both halves of the figure, but changing the size of the box makes the text on the right seem larger.

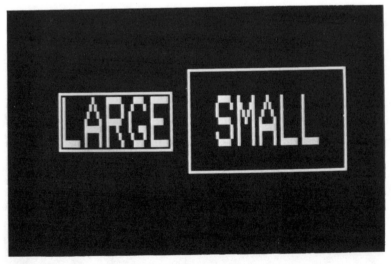

FIGURE 2-10. *Placement of Area Boundaries for Special Effects.*

Clearing Functional Areas

Virtually all CAI systems contain a primitive to erase the screen quickly. This primitive is often analogous to the "erase line" primitive, in that it may take the form of "erase from cursor to beginning of screen" or "erase from cursor to end of screen." With this type of primitive, positioning the cursor at the upper left-hand corner of the screen and executing the "erase from cursor to end of screen" primitive effectively erases the entire screen by turning all dots off.

Pop Erases

Erase screen primitives "pop" entire screen areas at once and create a distinct visual break. This break is often desirable, as in emphasizing the beginning or end of a discrete instructional unit. For maintaining visual continuity when erasing part of the screen, however, a *pop erase* is not the most appropriate technique.

Wipe Erases

The alternative to a pop erase is a *wipe erase*. This technique erases the screen more slowly and in a definite direction. The screen or area is erased like a chalkboard, as if someone passed an eraser over it.

Wipe screen erases are particularly useful for erasing functional areas in the shape of blocks. For example, consider the explanatory text area in Figure 2-4. This functional area begins on screen line 4 and extends down to line 13, and all text lines are displayed between screen columns 1 and 30. This area could then be wiped from top to bottom by excuting the following sequence of primitives:

1. Position cursor at line 4, column 30.
2. Execute the "erase from cursor to beginning of line" primitive. (The cursor remains in the same position.)
3. Move the cursor straight down to the next line, column 30. (This can usually be done by printing a line feed. ASCII character number 10.)
4. Repeat Steps 2 and 3 until line 18 has been erased.

Note that this technique could be used to erase a text block at the right of the screen by changing the "erase from cursor to beginning of line" primitive to "erase from cursor to end of line". However, both of these applications require that the functional area to be erased extend to one of the screen margins. They could not, therefore, be used to erase the simulated menu area in Figure 2-4 without also erasing the box that surrounds it. To erase only the menu options, you must use one of the techniques described below.

Wiping via Filling

On systems with only character cell level addressing, screen blocks that do not extend to one of the screen margins can be erased only by printing "space" characters into each character cell. On bit-mapped systems, however, you sometimes have a more sophisticated option if the system supports *filling* of a graphics area. Filling is a graphics characteristic that automatically draws a line from each point on a figure to another specified *filled point* or *fill line*. Consider, for example, the curves shown in Figure 2-11. All these curves are identical, but curve A was drawn without filling while curves B and C were drawn with filling. Note how the

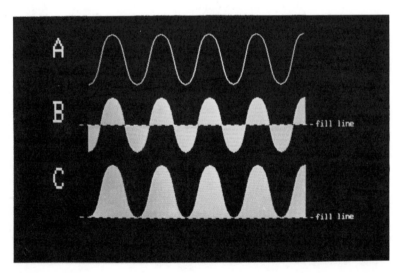

FIGURE 2-11. *Effect of Filling a Graphics Area With the Fill Line at Different Positions.*

shape changes from curve B to curve C as a result of moving the fill line.

Erasing a block on a bit-mapped terminal that supports filling can therefore be accomplished by defining the fill line to be the extreme bottom of the block area and then drawing a line across the extreme top. This technique will fill the functional area with a solid block the same color as the line being drawn. In systems that support erase mode as a primitive, drawing the line in erase mode effectively clears the entire block. (Erase mode is discussed in more detail in Chapter 5.) In less sophisticated systems, draw the line in the same color as the screen background (usually black) to achieve the same result.

Guiding the Student's Eye

As mentioned previously, all screen wipes have a characteristic direction. If used carelessly, this characteristic can be visually distracting because it can guide the student's eye to the wrong area of the screen.[3]

For example, consider once again the explanatory text block in Figure 2-4. Wiping this area from top to bottom and then rewriting it in the same direction provide two visual instances that guide the student's eye to the bottom of the area. The effect desired, however, is to guide the student's eye to the upper left-hand corner of the area where the text begins. It doesn't make much sense to write the text backwards from the bottom up, although some systems provide this capability as a primitive (so they can print languages such as Hebrew and Arabic). The effect of backward writing would be even more disconcerting than the undesirable eye guidance when writing the text in the normal fashion.

It does, however, make sense to wipe erase the screen from the bottom up or, in the case of bit maps with filling, from right to left. This technique was easily implemented for Figure 2-4 by making slight changes to the wiping technique described previously:

1. Position cursor at line 18, column 30.
2. Execute the "erase from cursor to beginning of line" primitive.
3. Move the cursor straight up to the next line, column 30.
4. Repeat Steps 2 and 3 until line 4 has been erased.

3. This problem was first pointed out to me by Wendy Mackay.

Using this technique, at least some of the screen changes guide the student's eye to the desired position, the top left-hand corner of the text block.

A Word About Text Display Rates

The discussion in Chapter 5 is devoted entirely to the display of text and the use of text as a graphics entity in itself, but one more point warrants mention here before closing the discussion of erasing and rewriting text areas. Virtually all computer/video CAI systems have the capability to display text much faster than students can read. All preceding arguments are predicated on the assumption that students wait until an entire text block is displayed before trying to read it. This assumption has proven true in my experience.

On the other hand, Alfred Bork (1982) has found that when students are allowed to control the rate at which text is displayed, they sometimes select rates that are extremely slow, even less than 30 characters per second. Such slow rates are definitely below the rate at which Bork's students can read, and his students may have selected these rates for reasons other than enhancing readability. For example, such slow display rates might strengthen the students' feelings that they are in control. Since most people who work with video displays for extended periods prefer maximum display rates, it is reasonable to assume that most students will prefer greater speed once they have become used to reading from a video display and are confident that the text will not be erased before they have had a chance to read it.

When a considerable amount of text must be displayed, however, some CAI authors have found it desirable to have the display pause to allow students to catch up. I do not prefer this technique personally, but Bork and others have used it effectively.[4]

A functional area issue equally important to display rates is display *order*. Once functional areas are erased, the order in which they are rewritten must be carefully planned. Graphics material should be displayed first, followed by any explanatory text. Otherwise, students might start reading the text and then be distracted as the computer draws a

---

4. The effectiveness of pausing was brought to my attention by Paul Blenkhorn.

complex figure. The directions should be the last entity displayed, possibly preceded by a brief pause. This will help assure that students read the screen instead of responding as quickly as possible just to get through the instruction.

Chapter Summary

The use of functional areas contributes clarity, consistency, and continuity to CAI screen design. Such characteristics make it easier for students to concentrate on the subject matter, because they reduce the amount of effort needed to understand the mechanics of the course itself.

CAI displays should contain a number of standard components:

- orientation information,
- directions,
- student responses,
- error messages, and
- student options.

A separate functional area is usually reserved for each of these components.

Functional areas can take any shape, but the easiest shape to work with is a rectangular block. Blocks suit themselves well to both text and graphics, and they are easy to erase with both pop and wipe techniques if properly positioned. When choosing where to locate functional areas on the screen, the designer must keep ease of clearing the areas in mind and consider the erasing primitives available. If information within a functional area is to be scrolled, this fact must also be considered when choosing specific area locations.

On terminals with only character cell level addressing, the easiest functional areas to clear are those that border on at least one of the screen margins. Pop erases clear a functional area instantaneously, while wipe erases clear the area more slowly and in a distinct direction which can be used to guide the student's eye. Use of both of these erasing techniques must be based on considerations of the overall visual effect desired.

Issues and Activities

1. The five standard screen components discussed in this chapter (orientation information, directions, student responses, error messages, and student options) are useful in many CAI courses. Consider a CAI course that you may have designed or would like to design. Would these standard components be useful in your course? If not, which ones should be eliminated? What other components might be needed to help students go through your course?

2. What special characteristics does your CAI system have for displaying orientation information and student options in a subdued manner?

3. Simulation programs can present special problems in providing students with directions, because the program author often does not want directions displayed to the student at all times. How might you implement directions and student options in this type of program?

4. If you have ever worked with any computer system, you have had experience with error messages. How would you rate the clarity and usefulness of the error messages you have seen? Did they give you all the information you needed to correct your mistakes? If not, how could they have been improved?

5. Review Activity 6 in Chapter 1. Would you change your assessment of the materials you reviewed after reading Chapter 2? How?

6. Figure 2-2 showed a number of standard CAI options. Which of these options would be easy to implement on your system, and which would be difficult? Consider the course you thought about for Activity 1 above. Which options shown in Figure 2-2 would you eliminate for that course? What other options would you add?

7. You have seen that blocks are the easiest shape to work with when setting up functional areas. Can you think of situations where an area in some other shape would be more appropriate?

8. What type of scrolling does your CAI system support? If it supports split screen scrolling, look up the commands to specify scrolling regions. Try making different combinations of lines scroll.

9. What type of erasing primitives does your system support? Try to implement one of the line wiping techniques introduced in this chapter.

10. If you have a bit-mapped terminal, find out whether it supports filling. If it does, write a program that draws a box on the screen, writes some text into that box, and then erases the text with a wipe via filling. Try wiping the area both horizontally and vertically.

11. Can you control text display rates on your system? If so, is such control useful for your students and the type of CAI lessons you plan to create, or should you just display text at the maximum rate?

·3·

Visual Symbols

A *symbol* is a visual entity that carries some specific meaning for students, just as a road sign carries some specific meaning for motorists. Symbols may be used:

- to indicate that the student is to perform a specific action, such as pressing the RETURN key;
- to identify a specific functional area, such as the directions;
- to tell the student that the system is busy performing some particular function;
- to abbreviate a wide variety of standard messages; and
- to build more complex graphics entities.

Virtually any graphics entity can be a symbol, but symbols are most often made up of single characters or a small set of characters. Letters are actually symbols, and so are the characters that make up the graphics character set that was shown in Figure 1-11. More commonly, however, symbols are thought of as small visual entities that convey a distinct meaning.

Symbols may be used on either bit-mapped or character cell systems. On most character cell systems, symbols must be built out of the existing character sets. On bit-mapped systems, however, CAI authors can usually define their own character sets. That is, these systems allow you to define dot patterns of your own design and associate each of these dot patterns with a letter. The complete set of your definitions forms a new character set.[1] By issuing a special command, you can put the system into a mode that will display your character set rather than either its standard or graphics character sets. This capability is very useful for displaying symbols and is discussed in the last part of this chapter.

This chapter begins with a discussion of the use of symbols to replace short, standard prompts. It explores the types of symbols that can be useful in CAI and looks at the design considerations for using them. The chapter concludes with an explanation of how a CAI author can create and use specialized symbols.

Uses of Symbols

Virtually all CAI materials have a number of points where students are told to press a specific key to go on to the next display. Even in the most sophisticated non-frame-oriented CAI programs, the first display often shows the program title and remains on the screen until the student presses a key to begin the program. In programs that prefer to use timing to advance from one screen to the next automatically, it is still a good idea to allow students to control screen advances occasionally to make sure that they are "in synch" with the program.

The PLATO system has a special key labeled "NEXT" that lessons commonly instruct students to press to advance to the next display. Other systems often instruct students to press the space bar or the RETURN key. In any case, it is important to understand that the "next" display need not erase the entire screen as in many frame-oriented programs. It might overlay part of the existing screen with new text or graphics, leaving part of the previous screen intact. Such systems typically display a message such as "Press RETURN to continue" somewhere on the screen. This was the intent of the message at the bottom of Figure 3-1, but that implementation proved to be an overkill. The large prompt in reverse video bordered with asterisks was so overbearing that it actually detracted from students' abilities to focus on the main parts of the screen. Later courses therefore used the shorter prompt shown in Figure 3-2.

1. Literature describing the Apple II℠ computer refers to user-defined character sets as *shape tables*.

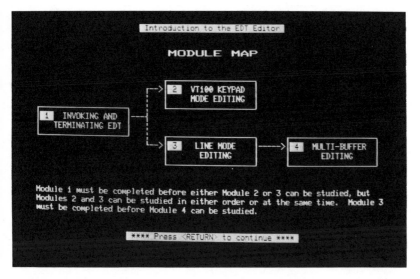

FIGURE 3-1. *An Overbearing "Press RETURN" Prompt.*

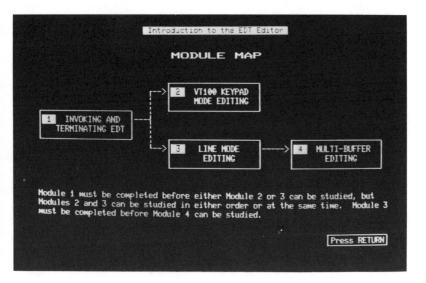

FIGURE 3-2. *An Unobtrusive "Press RETURN" Prompt.*

Figure 3-3 shows the quality of symbols that can be built on bit-mapped systems. This is a PLATO display, and each of the boxed words represents one of the special keys shown in Figure 2-3. Note how the

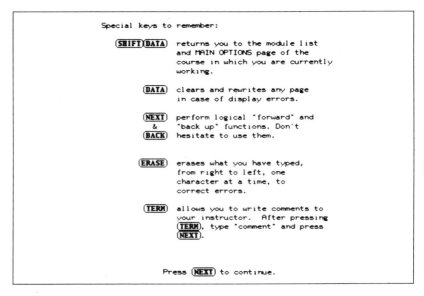

FIGURE 3-3. *High-Quality Key Symbols on the PLATO System. (Reprinted from* Control Data PLATO CMI System Overview, © *1978, 1979 by Control Data Corporation, by permission of Control Data Corporation. PLATO is a trademark of Control Data Corporation.)*

key symbols are differentiated from normal text. They are enclosed in boxes with rounded corners to make them look like keys, and the key names are printed in a *boldface* font with *serifs*. (Serifs are the fine lines that finish off the ends of the main letter strokes.) This amount of latitude for creating symbols is not usually available in systems with only character cell level addressing.

Another common need for a CAI prompt is to indicate that students are to type an answer. In some instances, the question can be displayed in such a manner that students simply type right after the question mark. This method is most useful on systems with large flashing cursors that draw students' attention to the question. But even on such systems, if students have been viewing a sequence of displays that only require pressing the RETURN key, it is often useful to provide some stronger type of visual clue that the system is now waiting for a more complex response.

The PLATO system has a built-in symbol designed specifically for this purpose. PLATO instructional developers call this symbol the "arrow," and it resembles a large right angle bracket (see Figure 3-4). Use of this arrow to indicate the need for a student response is extremely wide spread on PLATO. The symbol therefore has consistent meaning

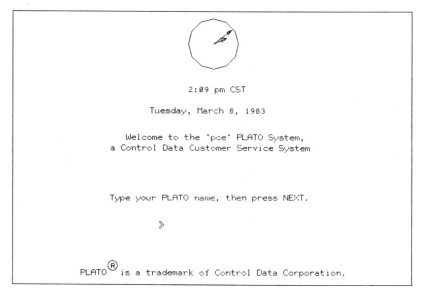

2:09 pm CST

Tuesday, March 8, 1983

Welcome to the "pce" PLATO System,
a Control Data Customer Service System

Type your PLATO name, then press NEXT.

PLATO® is a trademark of Control Data Corporation.

FIGURE 3-4. *The WELCOME TO PLATO Display from the Control Data Corporation PLATO System. Note the arrow prompt symbol. (Reprinted by permission of Control Data Corporation. PLATO is a trademark of Control Data Corporation.)*

across a very large number of courses and is familiar to virtually all PLATO students. It is an excellent example of a concise symbol that conveys a distinct message.

On complex screens, it is often useful to employ a symbol to identify the functional area for student directions, especially when this area is not adjacent to the area in which the cursor is waiting for input. This technique can help students locate the directions and, like the arrow symbol, indicate that they must do something other than simply pressing the RETURN key. In Figure 2-4, the symbol "→" was used to identify the student directions area. Figure 3-5 shows an even simpler symbol for this purpose, a solid block.[2] The course in which this symbol was used was very complex visually because it taught students how to program computer graphics. Functional areas shrunk and grew dramatically as various visual effects were demonstrated, and the directions were sometimes difficult to identify. The block was actually drawn in bright red on a color screen, and its consistent use throughout the course proved to be a helpful and effective visual clue.

---

2. The overall menu format shown in Figure 3-5 was designed by Roger Bowker.

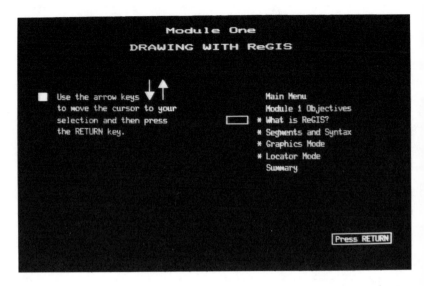

FIGURE 3-5. *Use of a Block Symbol to Identify the Functional Area for Student Directions.*

Almost any symbol can be used for any meaning, but students will find it much easier to remember symbols whose meanings closely match the visual images they convey. For example, the key symbols shown in Figure 3-3 are superior to the red block symbol shown in Figure 3-5, because the key symbols have intuitive messages while the red block itself has no intrinsic meaning. No matter how sophisticated the capabilities of your computer/video system, you must keep your students' intuition clearly in mind when designing symbols. It is usually better to use a simple symbol that is clearly meaningful to your students than to use a flashy one that students find ambiguous. You can best evaluate the clarity of your symbols by conducting *developmental tests* with your materials in rough form. This type of evaluation is discussed in Chapter 7.

The most important aspect of using symbols, however, is to use them consistently. The same symbol must have the same meaning at all times. For this reason, it is important to choose symbols that are not used within the context of your subject matter. Such ambiguity can seriously confuse students and impair their ability to concentrate on the subject matter.

Designing Symbols

Figures 3-1 through 3-5 illustrate a number of symbol designs. Some are exceedingly simple, while others are a bit more complex. As a general rule, it is best to keep symbols simple. A number of techniques can allow you to do this and maintain some elements of design as well.

Character cell systems usually offer little latitude in designing symbols. You are typically restricted to the standard and graphics character sets provided, and you must work within the limits of the character cell positions as well. Suppose, for example, that you wanted to represent the RETURN key as the word "RETURN" enclosed in a box. As shown at the left of Figure 3-6, this symbol on a character cell system would cover a screen area of three rows by ten columns. To get around this particular problem, you could display the word "RETURN" in reverse video as shown at the right of Figure 3-6, provided that the reverse video itself does not have some other special meaning or blend into a specific functional area. Note that when using reverse video, text usually looks better if you leave at least one blank space before and after the text.

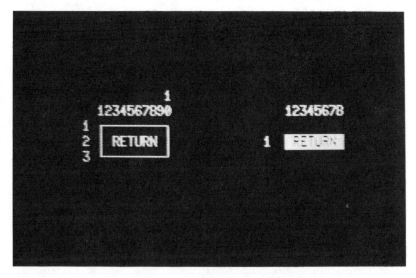

FIGURE 3-6. *Two Versions of a Symbol for the RETURN Key.*

Bit-mapped systems offer far greater flexibility. You can draw small pictures to use as symbols between the standard text lines. One of the simplest examples of these capabilities involves the use of arrowheads. Figure 3-7 shows the best that a system with only character cell level capabilities can do in representing the four standard keys for moving the cursor. Figure 3-8 shows what can be done on a bit-mapped system.

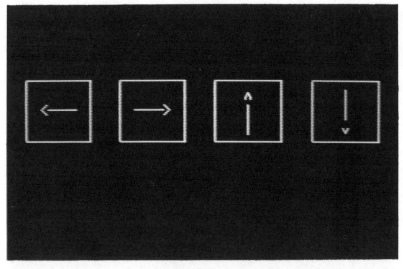

FIGURE 3-7. *Representation of Arrow Keys on a Character Cell System.*

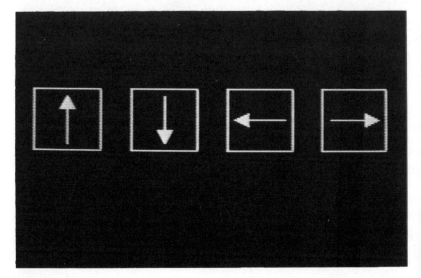

FIGURE 3-8. *Representation of Arrow Keys on a Bit-Mapped System.*

It is important to stress that you should not get carried away with designing pictorial symbols. For example, cuteness should usually be avoided at all costs. Cute symbols that appear again and again tend to become tiresome, especially if those symbols take longer to plot than normal characters. Some authors, of course, are experts at designing and using cute symbols that are not offensive to either children or adults. These authors generally use very simple pictures, like an octagon to represent a stopping point.

The biggest advantage of bit-mapped screens with regard to symbols is the ability to design your own character sets. Definable character sets have a large number of applications.

Definable Character Sets

Figures 1-10 and 1-11 showed that all characters are made up of dots. The pattern in which the dots are lit determines the symbol represented. For example, Figure 3-9 shows the pattern for a capital letter R in an 8 by 10 matrix overlaid with the corresponding bit map for this character. The areas where 1's appear (which would be individual pixels in an actual character) are turned on, while the areas where 0's appear are turned off.

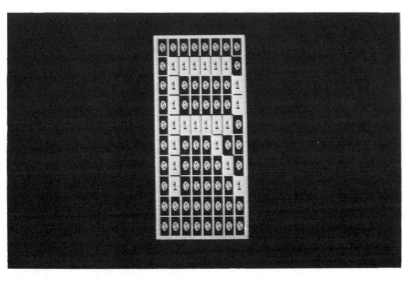

FIGURE 3-9. *Character Bit Map for a Capital Letter* R.

All systems have a special area of memory for storing the bit maps of their standard character set. This area is generally arranged in a linear table. When the system's video component receives an instruction from its computer component to display a specific character, the video component looks up the appropriate bit map in its table and turns the corresponding dots on or off as specified by the 1's and 0's.

One important point about this look-up and display process is that it is extremely fast. In effect, all of the dots in the pattern turn on simultaneously. This speed is a critical factor in the use of definable character sets for animation, and it will be referred to again near the end of this chapter.

Another important point about this process is that the table look-up is purely mathematical. The instructions to display characters sent by the computer system to the video system are encoded into numbers corresponding to locations in the character bit map table. For example, suppose the video display system receives an instruction to display character number 107 (decimal) in its table. With the normal character set loaded in the table, the bit map in this location would indicate the dot pattern for a lowercase "k." With the graphics character set loaded in the table, the bit map in location 107 might indicate the dot pattern for the top right-hand corner of a box. With your own character set loaded, the bit map in this location would represent some unique dot pattern that you have defined. Each dot pattern is displayed at the same fast speed, regardless of its complexity.

Character sets are defined by specifying the bit maps for each dot pattern you want to display. This process is unique to each computer/video system and can be complex. Fortunately, many systems provide a *character set editor* to simplify specification of the dot pattern. Such editors typically allow you to move the cursor around a simulated character cell enlarged for ease of viewing. You then press one key to add a dot at the pixel indicated by the cursor or another key to erase that dot. When the simulated character cell appears as you want it, a third key press tells the computer to translate your specification into the 1's and 0's needed for the character's bit map. The full set of character bit maps is usually stored on disk until a command is given to load it into the system's video component. The bit maps must be loaded into the video component's memory before they can be used to display your dot patterns.

Building Pictures from Character Sets

The characters you define can contain any dot pattern you find useful. As explained previously, the bit maps for all characters are simply series of 1's and 0's. They have no intrinsic meaning to the computer. You can therefore define characters that are actually parts of larger graphics entities and that, when put together in different patterns, can be used to form a variety of pictures.

One of the best examples of this application is a PLATO CAI program by Hyatt, Eades, and Tenczar (1972) that illustrates the different types of offspring generated when two fruit flies with different genetic traits mate. Figure 3-10 shows the dot patterns used to make up the

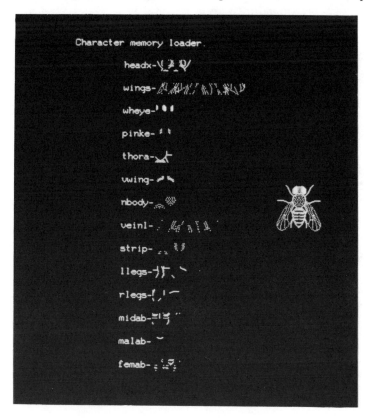

FIGURE 3-10. *Character Set for a Lesson on Fruit Fly Genetics. (Hyatt, Eades, and Tenczar, 1972.)*

character set for this program. (Note that PLATO's standard character cell size is 8 by 16.) If you look at these symbols carefully, you will notice that there are characters for pointed and rounded abdomens, full and degenerate wings, light and dark eyes, etc. Figure 3-11 shows how these characters were put together to display the four major types of fruit flies.

The use of the author-defined character set to draw the fruit flies has several advantages. First, it greatly simplifies the programming needed to display these pictures. Second, it makes the pictures modular so that any combination of wings and body shapes and eye types can be displayed. Third, it greatly increases the speed with which the pictures can be displayed. This third advantage is a critical point for animating symbols around the screen.

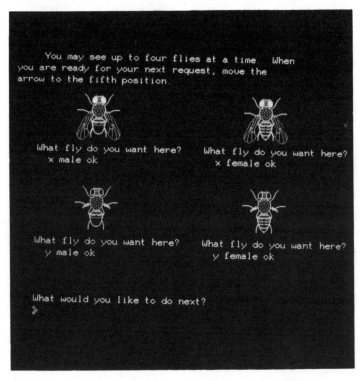

FIGURE 3-11. *Pictures Built From the Character Set in Figure 3-10. (Hyatt, Eades, and Tenczar, 1972.)*

Using Character Sets for Animation

All bit-mapped systems have commands for displaying dots and lines, but using these commands to display small complex symbols is at best tedious and at worst very slow. Consider, for example, the commands needed to display the symbol in Figure 3-12. This symbol is drawn in a 16 by 10 matrix with the upper left-hand corner positioned 200 pixels from the screen's left-hand margin and 100 pixels down from the top. Its starting position is therefore (200,100). (The first coordinate indicates the pixel column number and the second the row number.) To draw this symbol using line commands, the system must perform the following actions.

1. Position the cursor at (200,100).
2. Draw a line to (204,104).
3. Draw a line to (211,104).
4. Draw a line to (215,100).
5. Position the cursor at (200,109).
6. Draw a line to (204,105).

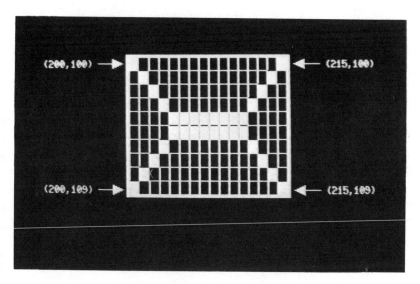

FIGURE 3-12. *Symbol Built Using a Character Set.*

7. Draw a line to (211,105).

8. Draw a line to (215,109).

Now consider the commands needed to display this symbol if the two halves of the symbol are stored in a character set:

1. Load the character set.

2. Position the cursor at (200,100).

3. Print the character corresponding to the left half of the symbol.

4. Print the character corresponding to the right half of the symbol.

This procedure is much faster than the line drawing procedure for two reasons. First, it obviously requires a smaller number of steps. Second, Steps 3 and 4 are extremely fast. The only problem with this procedure is that Step 1, loading the character set, can be quite slow on some systems. But if the symbol is going to be displayed often, the time spent loading the character set will be more than offset by the time saved during repeated displays.

Repetition is the key to *animation*. To make a symbol appear to move across the screen, you position the cursor, display the symbol, reposition the cursor one or two pixels away from the original position, and display the symbol again. The second display should overwrite and obliterate all the dots from the first one, completing the illusion that the symbol has moved. If this sequence of positioning the cursor and redisplaying the symbol is repeated fast enough, it effectively animates the symbol across the screen. The required speed is usually obtained by building the symbol as a character set rather than trying to draw it with line and point commands.

Character set animation was used very effectively in "How the West Was One + Three × Four," a PLATO arithmetic drill by Bonnie Anderson Seiler (Seiler and Weaver, 1974). Part of the character set defined by Seiler for this program is shown in Figure 3-13. When these characters are put together in the correct order, they display the stagecoach symbol in Figure 3-14. Animation of this symbol by the positioning and redisplaying technique described above results in the effect shown by the time exposure in Figure 3-15.

Note that Seiler's character set is designed so that the two extreme left columns of pixels turn all dots off. This is done specifically to obliterate these columns from the previously drawn symbol when the new

FIGURE 3-13. *Character Set for Building a Picture of a Stagecoach. (After Seiler and Weaver, 1974.)*

FIGURE 3-14. *Stagecoach Built Using the Character Set in Figure 3-13. (After Seiler and Weaver, 1974.)*

symbol is redrawn one or two pixels to the right. If the symbol had turned on any dots in the column farthest to the left, these dots would

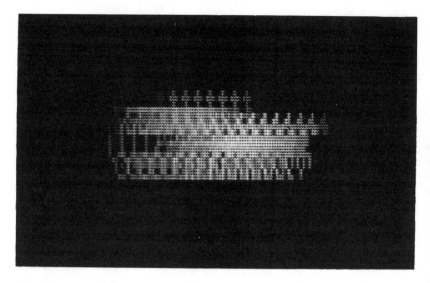

FIGURE 3-15. *Effect of Animating the Stagecoach in Figure 3-14. (After Seiler and Weaver, 1974.)*

have remained lit during the animation sequence, effectively leaving a trail behind the moving symbol. In most cases it is best to leave blank rows and columns around your entire symbol if possible so that it can be moved in an animated fashion in any direction. If you wish to leave a trail as the symbol moves along, it is usually an easy matter to display dots at the desired interval as a separate graphics operation.

Chapter Summary

A symbol is a visual entity that carries some specific meaning. Symbols may be used on either bit-mapped or character cell systems, but the former allow far greater latitude in designing symbols than do the latter.

In their simplest form, symbols are useful for adding emphasis to short, standard prompts. Symbols used in this manner should be kept simple and unobtrusive. In addition, it is usually advisable not to make them too cute, especially when dealing with adult students. Most importantly, symbols representing prompts to the student must be used in a consistent manner.

Symbol designs are highly dependent upon the capabilities of the screen. Character cell systems sometimes have graphics character sets to allow some creativity in symbol design, but the need to keep symbols small sometimes prohibits the use of these extended capabilities. On such systems, reverse video is often useful for setting a word symbol off from other text.

Bit-mapped systems not only allow the design of far more intricate symbols, they also allow symbols to be used in a much larger variety of ways by giving authors the capability to build their own character sets. Such character sets allow symbols to be used as building blocks for more complex pictures. In addition, the speed with which characters can be displayed makes it possible to do reasonable animation of small pictures.

Issues and Activities

1. Look at a number of CAI programs to find instances in which symbols are used. Can you identify the commands used to display these symbols? Are there other examples in the program in which symbols are not used but could have added clarity?

2. Analyze the symbols used in a particular CAI program. Are they clear? Are their meanings intuitive? Are they too overbearing? How would you improve them if you could?

3. If you have a character cell system with a graphics character set, find out all the different graphics characters you can display. If you have a bit-mapped system, find out whether you can define your own character sets and how this is done.

4. The PacMan® character in the popular arcade game is essentially a circle with a piece cut out. As this character moves across the screen, its mouth opens and closes, gobbling up dots, power pills, and ghosts. This action can be achieved by extending the cursor positioning and symbol display animation routine discussed in this chapter as follows:

   a. Load the character set.

   b. Position the cursor.

   c. Print the first character.

   d. Reposition the cursor.

e. Print the second character.

f. Repeat from Step b.

This routine effectively animates *two* characters at a time.

If you are working on a character cell system, animate the two characters "<" and "-" across your screen using the above routine. If you are working on a bit-mapped system, animate a solid circle and a solid circle with a piece cut out. (You will probably have to define the two circles in a character set to gain the required speed.)

The following exercises are for people with bit-mapped systems that allow them to define their own character sets.

5. Test the speed of plotting points with line and dot commands versus the speed of printing characters. Give your system the commands to display the symbol in Figure 3-12, and then define the two characters and display them. Which process appears faster? Make your system display the symbol by both methods 50 times. Now which process appears faster?

6. What is the character cell size on your system? Is there any way you can alter this size with special commands?

7. Acquire a CAI program or computer game that uses character sets for animation. How was the character set programmed? What techniques are used to animate the characters on the screen?

8. Does your system include a character set editor? If so, run the editor program and experiment with its capabilities. Does it provide access to all the character set features on your system?

9. "How the West Was One + Three × Four" includes a locomotive symbol as well as the stagecoach shown in Figure 3-14. Design your own locomotive or similar symbol and implement it on your computer/video system.

· 4 ·

Menus

A *menu* is a screen display designed to present students with a number of fixed options and allow them to choose the options they desire. Menus may be thought of as extended multiple choice points. They can provide a means for students to branch to various parts of a course and, if properly designed, they can provide a significant amount of orientation information as well.

This chapter introduces the concept of menus as student/computer interfaces and describes a number of ways in which menus can be used. It discusses design considerations for creating effective and efficient menu layouts and presents a number of different methods by which students may choose options from menus. The chapter concludes by presenting several ways in which students' choices may be visually represented on the screen.

The major problem when creating menus is trying to cram too much information onto a single screen. Consider, for example, the menu shown in Figure 4-1. At the top of the screen, this menu attempts to let students select a lesson to study in an instructional module. At the right, it lets students switch to one of the course's other three modules. At the bottom, it provides a number of additional options. The designer of this screen used a number of graphics techniques to separate the functional areas, but the visual effect is still one of crowded confusion.

This problem can often be solved by breaking a menu into two or more levels of menus. Each successive level is essentially an expansion of the one that preceded it. For example, the first level might list all the

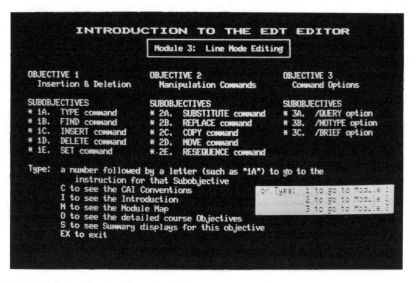

FIGURE 4-1. *An Overcrowded Menu.*

courses available in a curriculum. A set of second-level menus might then list the modules in each course, while sets of third-level menus list the lessons in each module. This type of structure is often referred to as a *tree,* because each successive level branches into a series of more precise menus. Such a structure is shown schematically in Figure 4-2. Using

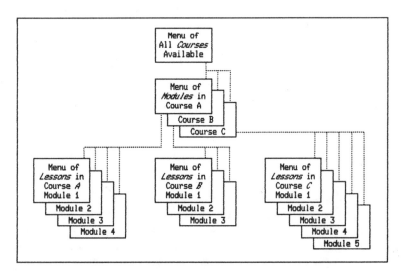

FIGURE 4-2. *Tree Structure for a Three-Level Menu.*

this scheme, the confusion in Figure 4-1 can be cleared up by the two menus in Figures 4-3 and 4-4.

You can get carried away with using menus just as you can get carried away with using symbols. As a general rule, tree structures should not require students to select options from more than three levels to

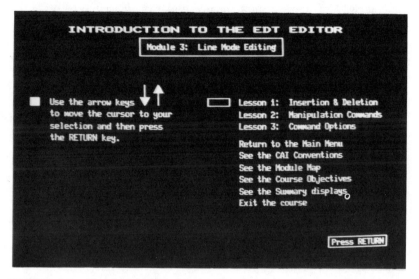

FIGURE 4-3. *Top-Level Menu for the Choices in Figure 4-1.*

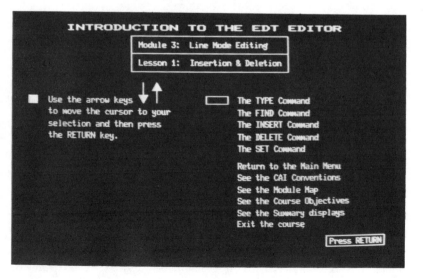

FIGURE 4-4. *Second-Level Menu for the Choices in Figure 4-1.*

completely specify what they are looking for. The need to progress through more levels quickly becomes annoying, especially if students have to wait for the screen to finish plotting before they can make their choices. In addition, more experienced students may find menus tedious if they believe they can specify what they are looking for in a more efficient manner.

One way to appease both novice and experienced students is to have all menu options available at all times. With this approach, the experienced students can request a specific menu option from any level, regardless of the menu level currently being displayed. The tree structure is still present, and can be displayed to guide the choices of less experienced students. Note that implementation of this functionality requires a unique typed request for each specific option throughout the entire tree. That is, you can't implement this functionality if you always expect students to type "1" for the first option on the screen, "2" for the second, etc., because the interpretation of these numbers changes as different menu levels are displayed.

Effective use of menus requires designs that are efficient, easy to use, and appropriate for both novice and experienced students. This chapter focuses on the design considerations relevant to achieving these goals.

Uses of Menus

Figures 4-1, 4-3, and 4-4 show the most common use of menus in CAI: selection of a lesson to study. Figure 2-4 shows a help menu that provides students with access to a number of additional course options. Menus can also be used effectively as parts of exercises, even though students may not even realize that they are working with a menu. This section presents further examples of these three applications and discusses some of their pros and cons.

Menus for Lesson Routing

Many CAI courses are set up as a series of *modules,* with each module containing one or more *lessons.* These divisions may be based simply on organizational convenience, or they may indicate specific *prerequisite* relationships between the modules to be studied. To illustrate the latter, consider the module map shown in Figure 4-5. Here Module 1 is intended to be studied first and Module 2 second. Once these two modules are completed, students may study Modules 3, 4, and 5 in any order, but all three of these should be completed before moving on to Modules 6 and 7.

Regardless of the reasons for which instructional divisions are established, a program can follow one of two strategies for *routing* students through the component modules. First, the prerequisite or some other logical module sequence can be imposed so that students are forced to go through the modules in a particular order. Alternatively, students can be allowed to devise their own routes through at least some of the modules, going from one module to any other at will. There is little need for menus in the first case, unless you wish to show students what they have done and where they are going. The second case, however, provides tailor-made applications for menus.

Menus for lesson routing are relatively straightforward and are now common features of most CAI programs with several component lessons. You simply need to display the names of the modules or lessons that students have access to and ask them to choose the one they want to study next. One problem encountered when designing routing menus of this type is limiting the number of levels students must go through

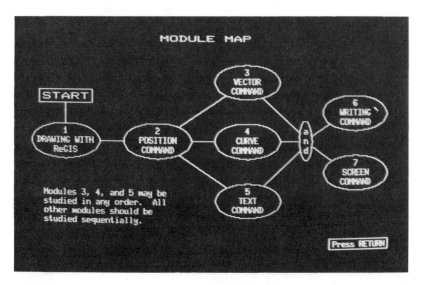

FIGURE 4-5. *Sample Prerequisite Relationships Between Modules.*

to specify their desired course section. The rule of thumb is to limit routing menus to a maximum of three levels.

Routing menus can provide significant amounts of orientation information, student control, and course branching. Chapter 2 addressed the problem of student orientation by suggesting use of a specific functional area for titles and subtitles. This approach is effective for letting students know where they are, but does little to orient them to the overall course structure. Menus can address this larger orientation issue by forming bridges from one part of a course to another.

For example, consider the menu in Figure 4-6. This menu orients students to the module being studied and lists this module's three component lessons. It also indicates that a higher level menu for the entire course exists. The design of this menu uses asterisks to mark completed lessons and a rectangular cursor to mark the next lesson to be studied. All in all, this represents a fair amount of orientation information in concise format, with much greater readability than the menu in Figure 4-1.

The degree to which students should be able to control their own learning is a sticky issue. Some educators feel that students should be given freedom to control as much as possible. These educators argue that such freedom increases motivation and enhances the adaptability

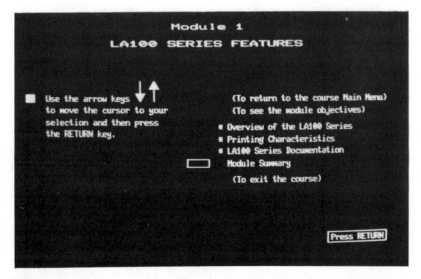

FIGURE 4-6. *A Concise Menu that also Provides Orientation Information.*

of programs to individual differences. Others believe that extensive control by students is inefficient because students don't really know how to use this freedom to explore their options effectively. You can reflect your own point of view by designing your menus to give students as much or as little control as you like.

Suppose, for example, you wish to use the menu in Figure 4-7 but choose to restrict students to following the prerequisite relationships specified in Figure 4-5. You can program the menu so that the cursor can only be moved next to those modules for which students had met the prerequisites, or you can display explanatory messages whenever students select modules for which they are not yet ready. Just because you list all of the modules in a course on a single menu doesn't mean that you have to let students choose them freely. However, this technique can tease students by showing them modules that they cannot yet select, so it must be used cautiously.

No matter how much you restrict control by students, any use of menus provides at least some branching in your course. The menus represent choice points and allow students' paths through your course to vary. Such branching may be easy or difficult to implement, depending upon your system. Large *time-sharing* systems typically have straightforward facilities for building courses as series of modules and lessons

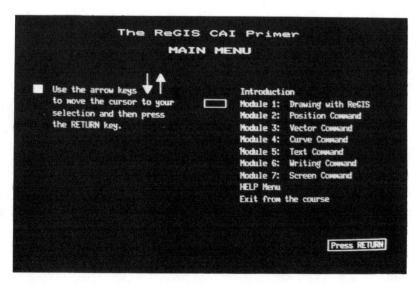

FIGURE 4-7. *A Menu for the Modules Specified in Figure 4-5.*

and for branching among the course segments. Small microcomputer systems may be a bit more difficult to work with in this regard and may require students to change diskettes before branching. Such obstacles can usually be surmounted by an experienced programmer. Design your routing strategy to be educationally effective, and then enlist the help of a programmer if you have difficulties implementing it.

Menus for Student Options

A number of desirable student options were introduced in Chapter 2, and one type of student options menu was shown in Figure 2-4. Systems dedicated to CAI sometimes have specially designed *function keys* for student options (Figure 2-3 shows PLATO's function keys). When such keys are present, there is usually little need for an on-screen menu.

Without special keys, however, students need to be prompted when special options are available. I once designed a system that required students to type single letter codes preceded by a left square bracket to select various options, such as "[H" for help, "[C" to enter a comment, and "[E" to exit (see Figure 2-2). I found, however, that students had trouble remembering this convention. The use of menus totally eliminates the need for students to remember codes. Menus provide a much cleaner student/computer interface and, like other effective screen design techniques, allow students to concentrate on the subject matter rather than on the mechanics of taking an on-line course.

The two major design issues concerning student options menus are when and where to display them. These menus may be displayed at all times or only after students press a HELP key. The choice is usually governed by the amount of screen area available for the menu and the number of options on the menu. Having the menu on the screen at all times can be distracting (especially for children), but if the menu is omitted altogether, students may often forget that they have additional options. This dilemma has caused some screen designers to opt for a simple "Help is available" message placed unobtrusively on the screen. Pressing the HELP key then calls in the full student options menu.

The issue of where to display student options menus is a screen layout problem, governed largely by decisions pertaining to functional areas. If the menu remains on the screen at all times, it should be positioned so that it does not interfere with the erasing primitives needed to clear other functional areas (see the discussion in Chapter 2 pertaining to Figure 2-7). If the menu appears only when students request it, it should be positioned so that it can be erased with a single primitive. A horizontally oriented menu on the bottom line of the screen (see Figure 2-4) satisfies both of these conditions, although other designs are possible.

Menus in Exercises

The menus discussed thus far have all been used to make it easy for students to respond when the system asks, "What do you want to do next?" The use of menus in exercises makes it easy for students to respond when the system asks, "Which of these choices is right (or wrong)?"

The simplest type of exercise menu, of course, is a multiple choice question. A typical menu of this kind is shown in Figure 4-8. (Note how students are notified about the availability of the additional options "Skip," "Quit," and "Review" on this screen.) In this case, students usually indicate their choices by typing letters or numbers corresponding to one of the available options.

Design of these menus is relatively straightforward, but two considerations exist for naive computer users. First, it is usually easier for

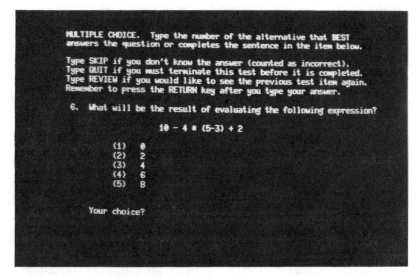

FIGURE 4-8. *A Multiple Choice Question Presented as a Menu.*

students without typing skills to find the first four number keys than to find the first four letter keys. Multiple choice questions should therefore label the options as 1–4 rather than A–D. (You may, of course, have more or fewer than four choices.) Second, it is often useful to program these menus so that students do not have to press the RETURN key after they've typed their responses. This speeds up the entire interaction considerably, but note that it does not allow students to correct their responses. This limitation is usually acceptable in an exercise situation, but you may wish to maintain the need to press RETURN in testing situations so students have a chance to change their minds.

Other exercise menus can be used much more creatively. For example, consider a screen that pictures the human heart coupled with an exercise that asks students to identify the four chambers. First, they are asked to identify the right ventricle, and a large cursor appears on the screen. Using the arrow keys, students move the cursor into what they think is the appropriate chamber and press a key such as RETURN. Their responses are judged right or wrong depending upon the position of the cursor.

Students going through such an exercise seldom realize that they are working with a menu. The menu options are actually defined as areas on the screen, and the program keeps track of the cursor's position by counting the number of key presses in each direction. For beginning students, the program might be written in such a way that the cursor can rest only in one of the four chambers. Feedback to students is then guaranteed to be either of the form "Yes, that's correct" or "No, that's the right aorta." For more advanced students, the cursor might move freely and more complex feedback might be necessary if they point to something other than one of the four chambers. Some systems provide devices such as light pens and touch-sensitive screens for student input on menus of this type. Use of these devices is discussed later in this chapter.

A final example of menu use in exercises pertains to simulations. A complex simulation might provide students with a large number of options that they must select quickly. Consider, for example, a medical simulation of an accident victim whose condition is quickly deteriorating. The goal, of course, is to stabilize the patient's condition and save his life. The display might show a number of the patient's vital signs, such as his pulse rate and blood pressure. Student doctors have a number of options available, including administering drugs or oxygen, performing cardiopulmonary resuscitation if the heart stops, calling for the patient's medical records, or perhaps even performing some kind of emergency surgery.

Since students need to think quickly, these options might be listed on the screen. Students might indicate the actions they wish to take in a number of ways, including typing straight English sentences to be analyzed by a sophisticated language interpreter. More commonly, however, each option will be preceded by a number that students can type to invoke it. The effects of that option on the patient's vital signs will typically be displayed on the screen, and students may be routed to a submenu to further specify what they want to do. (If they choose to administer a drug, for example, the system must find out which drug they wish to administer.) No matter how students indicate their choices, a menu will help keep them aware of their options. Again, this application may not resemble the menus discussed earlier in this chapter, but the program to drive such an exercise would vary only slightly from a program that asks students which module they wish to study.

Menu Layouts

The figures in this and the preceding chapters have shown a number of different menu layouts. Basically, the options can be arranged vertically, horizontally, or spatially (where each option is defined as a specific area of the screen). The considerations for each of these layouts are discussed below.

Vertical Layouts

All of the routing menus shown thus far have used vertical layouts, in which the options are listed one below the other in columnar form. This layout is generally the easiest for people to read, especially when each option contains three or more words.

Vertical layouts generally take up a lot of room, so they are best used when the menu is the major screen feature and can be given all the space it needs. Vertical layouts work even better when the menu is the only entity on the screen. In this case, the menu can be cleared easily with an "erase to end of screen" primitive. If you wish to wipe the screen rather than pop it, or if the screen contains other information that you want to retain, vertically oriented menus can be wiped with "erase to end (or beginning) of line" primitives if their functional areas extend to one of the screen margins.

Menus are meant to be used to indicate choices, so students typically do not read each option in its entirety. They scan the options for the one they want, read it to confirm its purpose, and then select it quickly. This action indicates that menu options should be worded with care to assure that they are discrete and nonambiguous. From a layout point of view, it also indicates that the text of the options should line up at the left—be *left-justified*—to help students scan them easily. Some designers like to center each menu option on a vertical axis, but this is much harder to scan. To see this for yourself, compare the two layouts in Figure 4-9.

Horizontal Layouts

Horizontal layouts, like the help menu strip shown in Figure 2-4, are particularly suited to situations in which:

• the menu is not the major screen feature,
• the overall screen image is to be preserved,

FIGURE 4-9. *Vertical Menu Layouts. The left-justified options at the top are easier to skim than the centered options at the bottom.*

- there are a small number of menu options, and
- each menu option can be limited to one or at most two words.

If any of these four characteristics is absent, a vertical layout may be the better choice.

Horizontal layouts don't leave much room for displaying the options. Standard industrial terminals usually provide a maximum of 80 characters per line, while most microcomputer displays provide only 40. Since you must leave at least one space (and preferably three spaces) as a separator between options, and often one of the options must be "Cancel" or "Exit" to return to the course, you just don't have much room for choices. But if the number of choices is small and each choice is but a single word, this layout can be used very effectively.

Since horizontal menus typically share the screen with course displays, it is best to set them off from the rest of the screen. This might be accomplished by printing the menu in reverse video as shown earlier, by printing it in a distinct color or type font, or by drawing lines to delineate it from the rest of the screen. No matter what visual technique you choose, it also helps to display the menu in the same functional area each time. This helps to identify the menu and to maintain students' orientation to the program's mode.

Spatial Layouts

Spatial layouts are menus in which each option is actually defined by a bounded screen area. This is the type of menu that was discussed in the heart chamber example in the "Menus in Exercises" section. This layout, by its very nature, can be used only when a substantial part of the screen can be devoted to the menu.

Programming of spatial menus can be difficult if your system has no specific facilities to make the task easier, but experienced programmers can usually help you solve the implementation problems. Even with experienced programming help, however, the design problems with spatial menus are significant.

The first design problem is to determine the minimum screen size for each option. On systems where students will indicate their choices by moving a cursor, the minimum physical size is either one character cell or one pixel, depending upon the level of control students have over the cursor. But these physical minimums are seldom, if ever, practical to use. It is better to make the size of the option several times the physical minimum so that students can move the cursor quickly and "hit" their choice with a reasonable amount of latitude.

Systems that use light pens or touch-sensitive screens require relatively large areas for each option. (These devices are discussed in more detail later in this chapter.) This requirement seldom presents a problem, because spatial menus typically take up most or all of the screen. Designers must, however, keep the input medium in mind and position the options far enough apart to avoid erroneous "hits."

The second design problem with spatial menus is to decide how much tolerance you will allow around the target area for each option. In discussing the heart chamber identification exercise, I mentioned that the menu might be programmed so that the only available cursor positions are squarely and clearly in one of the four chambers. In this case, there is no need to worry about tolerance.

In the more sophisticated situation in which the cursor moves freely, however, you must decide just how far within each chamber you require students to point. If the target area is too small, students may quickly become frustrated trying to hit it. But if it is too large, the probability of an erroneous hit is greatly increased. The best solution is to define target areas just slightly smaller than you are comfortable with at first, and then program helpful error messages for students who miss these areas. For example, instead of just saying, "No, please try again," have the error message read, "I can't decide if you are pointing to the upper right- or left-hand chamber. Please move the pointer closer to the center of one of the chambers."

Choosing Options

Once a number of menu options have been displayed on the screen, you must provide a way for students to choose the options they desire. The very simplest way to do this from a programming point of view is to ask students to type the options they desire. But this technique is not satisfactory for students who have trouble typing, especially if the menu options are long. Three other "human-engineered" methods are available:

1. the use of numbers and keywords,
2. the use of arrow keys, and
3. the use of touch sensitive screens, light pens, etc.

Each of these is applicable to a different system, depending upon the system's individual capabilities.

Entering Numbers or Keywords

One way to get around the typing problem is to number each item and have students type the numbers representing the options they have chosen. This strategy is very easy to program, but it is subject to error by students and has the added disadvantage of giving the computer interaction a numerical flavor.

A better way to solve the problem is to let students type abbreviations of the options or specific *keywords* for each option. A keyword is a single word in an option that serves to represent that option. Consider, for example, the menu shown in Figure 4-10. Here the keywords for each option are shown in italicized type. Note that the words chosen to be the keywords are short, distinct, and representative of the entire option.

Now consider the effect of rewording the options in Figure 4-10 to those in Figure 4-11. Here the keywords are positioned as the first words in each option. This arrangement has distinct advantages for students because it makes it logical for them to indicate their choices by typing one or two letters, just enough to identify uniquely the option they

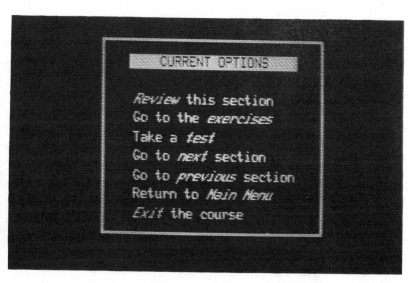

FIGURE 4-10. *Italicized Keywords in Menu Options.*

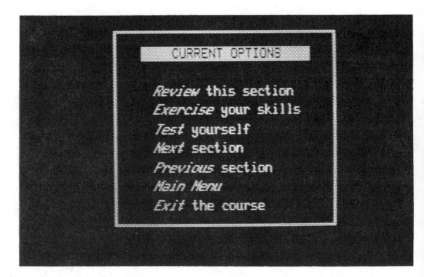

FIGURE 4-11. *Rewording of Options in Figure 4-10 to Position Keywords at the Beginning of Each Option.*

choose. In addition, the left-justified position of the keywords makes them easy to scan.

Keywords are probably the clearest means for students to indicate their choices without ambiguity or high probability of error when the only way for them to choose options is through the keyboard. The method can be used with both vertical and horizontal layouts and is natural and efficient.

Using the Arrow Keys

Most computer/video systems provide considerably more possibilities than just typing for selecting options from menus. One that is particularly suitable for children as well as older students is to provide a pointer that they can move around with the arrow keys. This technique requires a bit more programming effort than keywords, but it doesn't require any typing at all by the student.

Most of the menus illustrated allow students to choose options using the arrow keys. In Figures 4-6 and 4-7, the arrow keys are used to move a small flashing box next to the desired option. In the horizontally oriented help menu in Figure 2-4, the arrow keys cause the next option to the left or right to be marked by changing it from reverse video to standard video. In spatially oriented menus, use of the arrow keys is usually required due to the nature of the task. You see, therefore, that the arrow keys can be used in a variety of ways and that their use is applicable to virtually all types of menus.

It is important to point out that the two techniques discussed so far are not mutually exclusive. That is, there is no reason why both methods for choosing options can't be operational simultaneously so that students at different levels can use whichever method is more comfortable. This point is important for systems designed to be easy for non-typists, because such systems are typically awkward for people who touch-type. Accomplished typists generally like to keep their fingers on the "home" keys (ASDF and JKL;) and find it distracting to move their hands to special function keys positioned at the side. Combining the keyword and arrow techniques usually makes everybody happy, and implementing both is usually just slightly more difficult than implementing one.

Using Touch-Sensitive Screens, Light Pens, Etc.

The PLATO system has had a touch-sensitive screen for over a decade. The actual hardware method for making the screen touch-sensitive has changed over the years, but the ease of using this type of capability for choosing options from menus cannot be equalled. A number of very clever programs have been implemented using the touch-sensitive screen, particularly exercises with spatial menus.

A number of devices are now on the market that allow students to point at the screen:

- A *light pen* is a wand-like device whose position can be detected by the system when it is pointed at the screen.
- A *graphics tablet* (also called a *bit pad*) is a rectangular board that can detect the position of an electronic stylus placed on it.
- A *mouse* functions like the stylus on a graphics tablet, but no special board is required. The mouse is simply moved over a flat surface and one or more wheels on the bottom send signals to the computer so that it can detect how far the mouse has moved and in which direction.
- *Paddles, joy sticks,* and *tracker balls* are all devices that video game fans are familiar with. They operate in similar ways, basically transmitting signals that the computer interprets as instructions to move a pointer in various directions.

All of these devices can be used to move pointers or otherwise indicate choices on menus. Systems that provide them usually provide relatively simple software facilities for using them, so they do not present any particular programming problems. Students generally find using these devices fun, and their use can greatly speed up students' interactions with menus.

The devices listed above are particularly well suited to choosing options on spatially oriented menus. Several advanced systems, however, have also demonstrated that they can be effective interfaces for other types of vertical and horizontal menus as well. The key to using them in these applications is to match them with the overall course strategy. That is, if a PLATO course makes no use of the touch-sensitive screen while teaching the subject matter, there is probably little reason to make the routing menus touch-sensitive except as a gimmick. But if a light pen or mouse is an integral part of the instructional part of a course, its use might also be incorporated into the routing menus. Note again that adding the functionality for such devices does not exclude the functionality for keywords and arrow keys. It should merely provide an alternate input method for students who find it easier.

Indicating Students' Choices

The final task in menu design is to decide how you will indicate the option that the student has chosen. In some systems the choice of technique is obvious. For example, if students use the arrow keys to move a pointer or cursor, the pointer or cursor itself will indicate the option they have chosen.

If they select an option by typing a keyword, however, the choice may not be as obvious. In this case, an effective technique is to highlight the option by changing its video attribute from normal to reverse video or vice versa. This technique is particularly suited to horizontal menu layouts in which the menu itself is printed in reverse video to distinguish it from the main screen display. As stated earlier, horizontal layouts provide little room for the options themselves, so virtually no room at all is left for adding pointers to the options. Changing the active option from reverse to normal video clearly distinguishes it from the others and requires no additional space.

A similar highlighting technique is to rewrite the selected option in boldface. This text attribute is not available on many bit-mapped systems, but it should not be overlooked on the systems that do provide it. Reverse video has so many applications (such as displaying blocks and putting boxes around other graphics entities) that it is often used for a number of different purposes on the same screen. A different technique, like using boldface, is therefore helpful for avoiding visual confusion with other uses of reverse video.

Color can also be used to highlight menu options and is more commonly available than boldfacing. Suppose, for example, that you decide to lay out your help menus horizontally and print them in blue text. You might then indicate in yellow the option chosen by the student. You will want to pick two strongly contrasting colors for this technique, but this should not be difficult unless you have already set up conventions for color usage in other text. If you have already set up conventions, try to stick to the same color scheme you use elsewhere to avoid using the same color with different meanings in different situations.

One video technique that is *not* recommended for indicating students' choices is *blinking* or *flashing*. This is a very powerful visual technique and catches the eye so strongly that it is hard to read other material on the screen. Blinking is simply overbearing for indicating students' choices and should be reserved for applications in which use of its strong eye attraction is more warranted.

Chapter Summary

Menus represent an extremely important screen design technique because they can be applied to such a large variety of student/computer interactions. They can be used to route students through a modular course, provide additional input options, and simplify the ways in which students indicate responses to exercises.

The main considerations in designing menus are:

1. how many options they should include,
2. how the options should be laid out on the screen,
3. how students should choose the options they desire, and
4. how their choices should be indicated visually.

The number of options can be controlled by breaking large menus into a number of submenus. Options layout depends largely on the menu's size and purpose; vertical, horizontal, and spatial layouts are possible. The manner of choice depends largely on the extent of input devices that students have available, such as arrow keys, touch-sensitive screens, light pens, etc. Visual indication of options depends partially on the visual capabilities of your screen, but is more often determined by the nature of the menu and the style in which students choose options.

Issues and Activities

1. Using Figure 4-2 as a model, construct a menu tree for a CAI course in your major subject area. What skills would you group together for each lesson? Which lessons fit together to form modules? Design menus to allow students to move up and down your tree.

2. What are the prerequisite relationships between the major skills you teach? Assign each skill a number and draw a diagram similar to the one in Figure 4-5 to indicate their relationships.

3. Assuming that you had a full complement of CAI lessons covering a specific subject area, how much control would you exercise over your students' abilities to gain access to those lessons? Are your students the type who should have access to all lessons at all times, or would it be better to restrict access in some way? If you did want to restrict access, how might you accomplish it?

4. Does your system have any special function keys? If so, are their functions preprogrammed and immutable, or can you use them to allow access to student options?

5. Study a number of CAI lessons that make use of menus. Are the menus well designed? How might you improve them?

6. Design a menu similar to that in Figure 4-11. Experiment with your system's different capabilities for highlighting the keywords.

7. Are vertical or horizontal menu layouts easier to implement on your system? Which techniques for choosing the options work best with your students?

8. Can you implement spatial menus on your system? If so, what facilities exist for students to indicate the screen area they have chosen?

9. Does your system have a touch-sensitive screen, a light pen, or other similar feature? If so, how might students use this feature to select options from menus?

10. What features does your system have for indicating students' choices? Which one works best with each of the three different menu layouts (horizontal, vertical, and spatial)?

·5·

Text Display

Today's computer/video systems can communicate messages to students via three basic channels: sound, graphics, and text. Very few CAI systems currently have effective integrated sound systems, although there are some notable exceptions. These exceptions generally use sound for music education, generating organ-like tones rather than spoken messages (see, for example, Hofstetter, 1975). Speech synthesis systems do exist, but are not in widespread use for CAI. Perhaps the most promising systems for integrating audio messages with CAI are those that are tied to videodiscs. These relatively new systems can often control two separate sound tracks independently, playing them individually or together to generate stereo. In addition, some of these systems allow the sound tracks to be played without displaying pictures from the videodisc. These systems make it possible to use pre-recorded sound as a communication channel with standard computer displays.

Although I have emphasized and demonstrated the communication power of graphics and pictures throughout this book, particularly in Chapter 3, Visual Symbols, the examples really just scratch the surface as far as computer graphics are concerned. Generating pictures by computers is a large topic area that is well beyond the scope of this discussion. While the use of graphics can be crucial to effective CAI screen design, the widely varying capabilities of currently marketed machines make it difficult to establish stringent guidelines on how graphics should or should not be used. At this point I can only present you with a number of examples, implore you to experiment with the capabilities of your own system, and encourage you to rely on your own artistic and creative senses to help you use these capabilities effectively.

Text display techniques, on the other hand, are relatively standard from one computer/video system to the next. The ways in which different systems can display text are similar, as are the commands used to achieve various effects. In addition, text remains a major communication vehicle on virtually all CAI systems, even those with extensive graphics capabilities. The study of text display techniques is therefore an important component of CAI screen design.

This chapter demonstrates the importance of wording text messages for clarity. It explores the effects of various text layouts on readability and discusses the uses and abuses of a large number of text attributes. The final section reviews different ways in which text can be displayed on video screens.

Message Clarity

The first consideration in using text (or any communication channel for that matter) is to assure that the message you are trying to convey is clear. Given the special nature of computer/video systems, a large number of techniques are available for formatting text and emphasizing certain keywords. But no visual technique can compensate for messages that are poorly written.

Consider, for example, the following scenario. A CAI system is built to accommodate a number of students and record data on each student's work individually. The system includes a registration program that asks students to identify themselves by typing their "code names," secret passwords they have selected specifically for this purpose. Students who have not yet registered on the system (and therefore do not have code names) are directed to press the RETURN key without typing anything else. This action causes the system to branch to an auxiliary registration program which leads students through selecting their code names. The system then stores the new code names for use in future registrations.

My first attempt at directing students to either type their code name or press the RETURN key alone is shown in Figure 5-1. This display provides an important lesson in message clarity, because it turned out to be the most difficult hurdle in the entire CAI system. The directions simply didn't get their message across, and both possible types of mis-

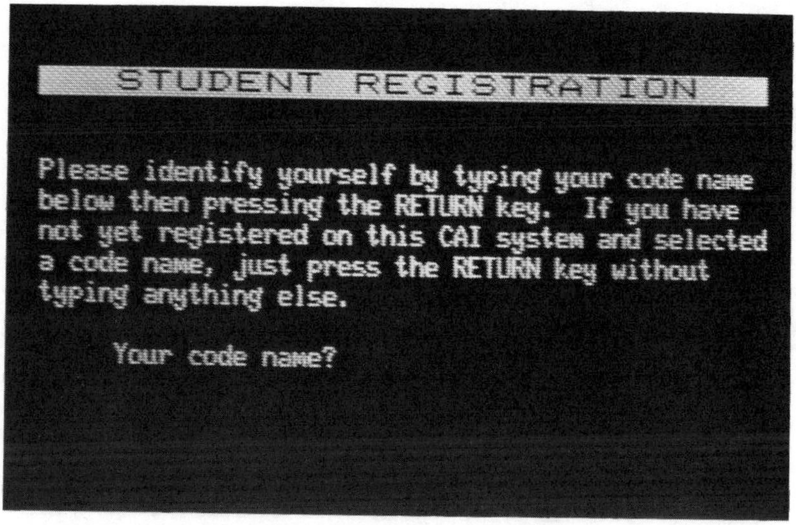

FIGURE 5-1. *Student Registration Display, Version 1.*

takes were made: new students tried to type code names and previously registered students pressed only the RETURN key.

By observing students as they wrestled with these directions, my colleagues and I learned that new students made far more errors than previously registered ones. The action required of new students was therefore emphasized by enclosing their directions in a box and rewording them as shown in Figure 5-2.[1]

The box helped considerably, but we felt that the instructions were still too wordy. The form was therefore streamlined further as shown in Figure 5-3.[2]

The error rates with this form were far less than with the original, but some students still became confused. The distinction between the new students and previously registered students was therefore stated explicitly as shown in Figure 5-4.[3]

These figures show a steadily increasing use of graphics to clarify the basic message conveyed by the text. This trend is not accidental. As discussed in Chapter 3, Visual Symbols, text and graphics can often be used to complement each other, and their combination typically con-

[1]. This refinement was made by Roger Bowker.
[2]. This refinement was made by Wendy Mackay.
[3]. This refinement was made by Jack Jurras.

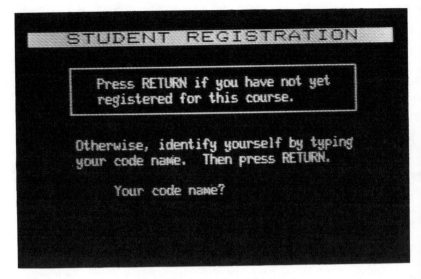

FIGURE 5-2. *Student Registration Display, Version 2.*

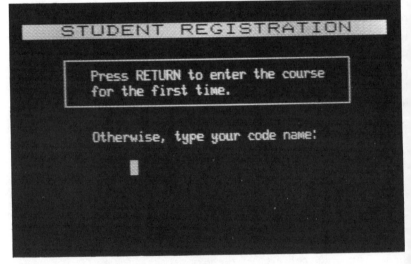

FIGURE 5-3. *Student Registration Display, Version 3.*

veys a far clearer message than either technique used alone. For example, consider the strength of the messages conveyed by road signs: the symbol ○ clearly represents "stop" (at least to American drivers), but the symbol ◇ represents "caution." They text inside the caution symbol

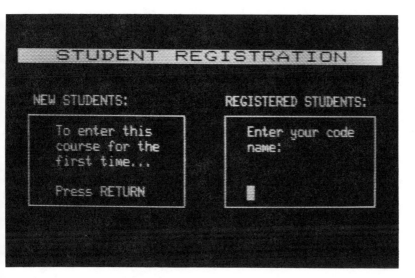

FIGURE 5-4. *Student Registration Display, Version 4.*

nforms drivers of the type of danger they face.

While no screen design techniques can substitute for well-written text, graphics and symbols can be used to clarify and punctuate a message's meaning. It is always best, however, if the text of your messages can stand alone. There are two simple ways to test the quality of your messages. First, try reading the text aloud. If you stumble over any of the words, chances are your students will, too. Second, observe students directly as they try out your materials. Watch their faces for any signs of confusion. If two or more students appear to have trouble with any single message or instruction, that display is probably in need of revision. (This type of observed trial is often referred to as *developmental testing* and is discussed further in Chapter 7.)

Message Readability

Message clarity is a prerequisite to the success of any text communication. Given this clarity, a number of other factors contribute to the readability of the text on the screen. These factors are:

- type style,
- line length,

- justification, and
- break points,

each of which is discussed below.

Type Style

The use of boldface and serifs was introduced in Chapter 3. These characteristics represent embellishments to type styles and are generally used on computers only to emphasize keywords or symbols. Standard type styles, or *fonts*, possess a number of different characteristics that contribute directly to the readability of text displayed in these fonts.

The fundamental characteristic of any text display is the presence of lowercase letters. All systems provide uppercase display capabilities, but some of the smaller systems currently being used for CAI do not provide lowercase as part of their basic hardware or software package. Lowercase is a strong contributor to readability, as you can see by comparing the two bodies of text in Figure 5-5. Many bit-mapped systems that do not include lowercase (such as the basic Apple II) allow you to create a lowercase character set via the techniques discussed in Chapter

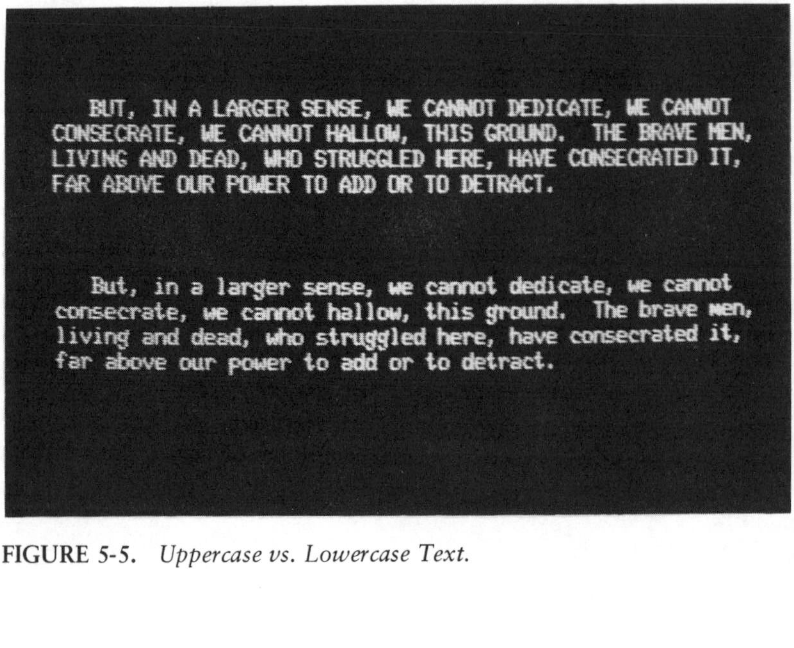

FIGURE 5-5. *Uppercase vs. Lowercase Text.*

3. This technique should be used whenever possible due to its positive effect on readability.

Some systems that do provide lowercase letters do so poorly. The main measure of quality in this regard is the presence of *descenders* on the letters g, j, p, q, and y. The descender is that part of the letter that "goes below the line" on which the letter is written. Figure 5-6 compares the quality of text in two type fonts, one with descenders and one without.

My experience is that the effect of descenders on readability varies with the target population, and in a manner that is counterintuitive. That is, one would generally expect children to be more seriously affected by this anomaly than adults, because the letters don't look like those they've been taught. Children do have trouble recognizing these letters the first time they see them, but once they are told what the letters are and that the strange style is "just the computer's way of writing," they tend to adapt very quickly. Adults, on the other hand, seem to be quite put off by the malformed letters and can actually get hung up to the degree that their reading ability is seriously impaired.

Unfortunately, systems with poorly formed lowercase letters seldom allow you to define your own character sets, so you must either live with the problem or use another display system. The bottom line is that

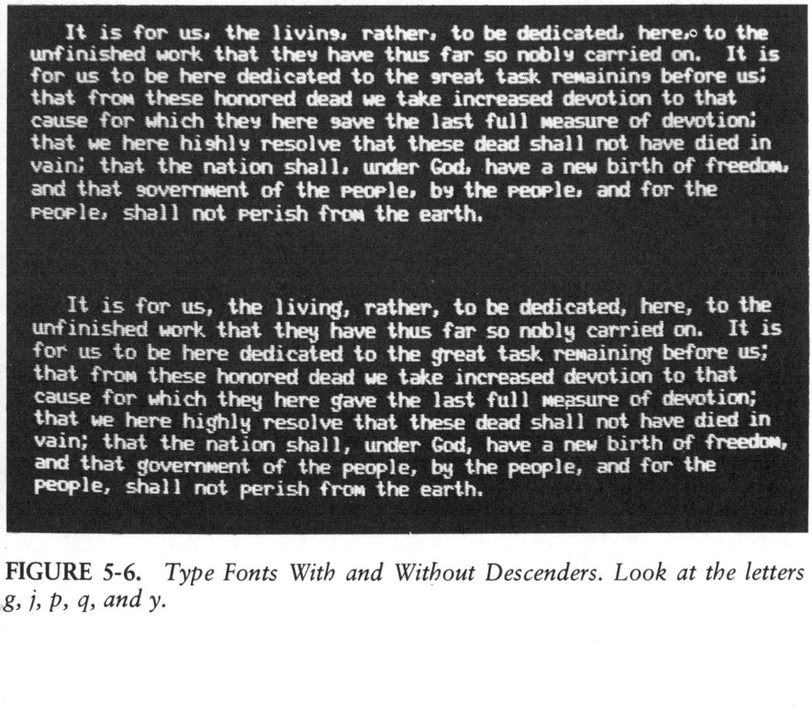

It is for us, the living, rather, to be dedicated, here, to the unfinished work that they have thus far so nobly carried on. It is for us to be here dedicated to the great task remaining before us; that from these honored dead we take increased devotion to that cause for which they here gave the last full measure of devotion; that we here highly resolve that these dead shall not have died in vain; that the nation shall, under God, have a new birth of freedom, and that government of the people, by the people, and for the people, shall not perish from the earth.

It is for us, the living, rather, to be dedicated, here, to the unfinished work that they have thus far so nobly carried on. It is for us to be here dedicated to the great task remaining before us; that from these honored dead we take increased devotion to that cause for which they here gave the last full measure of devotion; that we here highly resolve that these dead shall not have died in vain; that the nation shall, under God, have a new birth of freedom, and that government of the people, by the people, and for the people, shall not perish from the earth.

FIGURE 5-6. *Type Fonts With and Without Descenders. Look at the letters g, j, p, q, and y.*

if you design your own lowercase character set, include descenders. If you are using a terminal with lowercase that doesn't have descenders, try to switch it with one that does.

One sophisticated text characteristic that is available on some systems is variable letter widths. On systems with this characteristic, letters such as k and d are wider than i and l, but not quite as wide as w and m. The font used in this book demonstrates variable letter widths, as do most typeset materials. Although this technique can be abused by making the variations in width too great, a font with variable letter widths is generally pleasing to the eye and promotes readability. Variable letter widths on computer systems are generally implemented through software rather than hardware, so it is theoretically possible to give any bit-mapped system this capability. The process is rather complex, though, and few designers try to program it themselves. One generally has to look at expensive systems to find the technique used, but Bell & Howell have done a nice job of integrating it into the standard features of PASS®, their Professional Authoring Software System for the Apple II.[4] A sample of text with variable letter widths is shown in Figure 5-7.

FIGURE 5-7. *Variable Letter Width Font Used on the PASS® System.* © 1983 *by Deltak, Inc. used with permission.*

4. PASS® is a registered trademark of Bell & Howell Co.

Line Length

After text style, the second most important factor in readability is line length. In general, the shorter the line, the easier it is to read. Long lines require excessive eye movement and make it difficult for readers to move their eyes smoothly from the end of one line to the beginning of the next. The problem is exaggerated when type sizes are small. This is why newspapers and magazines are printed with several columns per page. The multicolumned layout allows them to keep their text size small and thus save paper while keeping line lengths short and making their text easy to read.

Type size and line length go hand in hand. Guidelines for line lengths are therefore generally expressed in numbers of words rather than linear measure. A good rule of thumb for printed materials is to limit the number of words per line to approximately the reader's age until you hit the teens. For computer screens, the lines should be even shorter, perhaps a maximum of eight to ten words per line for adults. The reason for this rather conservative guideline is that reading text from a computer screen is considerably more difficult than reading it from a piece of paper. The resolution is lower, the angle of view is less comfortable, and the luminous nature of the screen can put more strain on the eye. All of these factors speak in favor of short lines.

The desirability of short line lengths is sometimes used as a justification for screens that allow only 40 characters on a single line, but this justification is indefensible. As many of the figures in this book have shown, just because a screen allows 80 or even more characters per line does not mean that you have to display your text in that format. It is often desirable to display text and graphics simultaneously or to display text in a narrow column within a screen area reserved for a specific function. Wider screens allow this flexibility, while narrow screens generally do not (or make it difficult). So if you have the option, use as wide a screen as possible, but consider readability when defining the width of your text areas.

Justification

Justification is a property of text margins. Margins that are aligned are said to be *justified,* while margins that are not are said to be *ragged.* All of the text in this book is left-justified (the left margin is straight) as well as right-justified. This format is standard for books, magazines and newspapers and is generally easy to read with typeset text. Justification on computer screens, however, possesses altogether different characteristics.

Consider the qualities of typeset text that make justification of both margins aesthetically pleasing in books. First, typeset text has variable letter widths. This characteristic trains the eye to take in different amounts of information (numbers of letters) in similar horizontal distances. Second, typeset text has *kerning,* the overlapping of letter combinations such as AV and LY so that the apparent inter-letter distances are the same as those between other pairs of letters in the font. Third, typesetting allows small additional spaces to be added between all adjacent letters in a line so that the line expansions needed to achieve left- and right-justification simultaneously are hardly noticeable.

Notwithstanding the avant-garde look of right-justified text with ragged left margins and the highly graphic text styles used in advertising, doubly justified text has a distinctively "professional" look. For this reason, many designers like to try to justify text on computer screens. But the effect on a screen is totally different from the effect on paper because most screens possess none of the three qualities listed in the preceding paragraph.

The most significant shortcoming of justification on computer screens is the inability to add small spaces between letters. (Like variable letter widths, this capability can be implemented on bit-mapped screens via software, but the programming effort is appreciable.) Thus the only way to expand lines to achieve right justification is by adding whole spaces between words. As shown in Figure 5-8, the effect of this technique is not generally pleasing, and the large variations in spacing seriously impair readability. Note also that short text lines generally exacerbate the justification problem by limiting the number of inter-word spaces where additional space can be added.

Gregory and Poulton (1970) have found that while good readers are not generally affected by unattractive text formats, poor readers have significantly poorer reading comprehension when text is doubly justified. The peculiar thing about justification, of course, is that it is generally more difficult to implement than leaving one margin ragged. Given its detrimental effect on readability, it is perhaps difficult to understand why anyone would go to the trouble. But a large number of screen displays can be found with justified text, so it appears worthwhile to lobby strongly against its use.

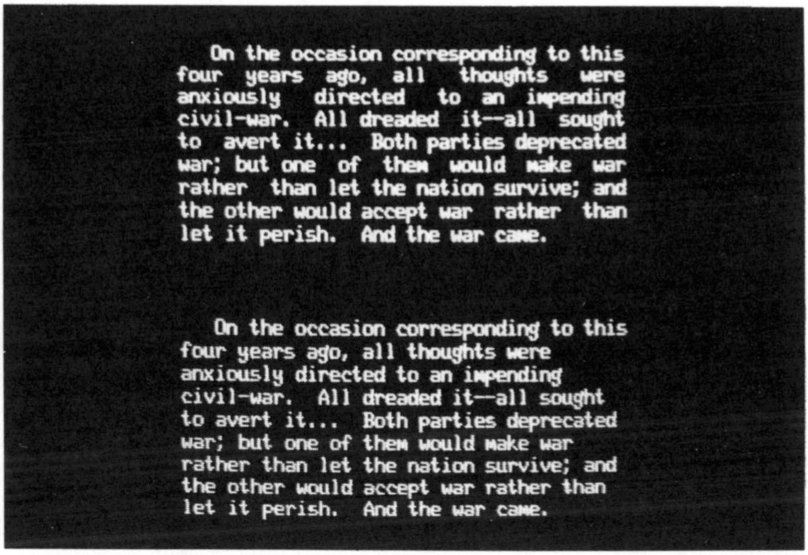

FIGURE 5-8. *Justified and Ragged Text.*

Break Points

Chapter 1 cited a number of important ways in which the computer/video medium differs from the printed page. One of these ways involves the cost of blank space: it has an identifiable cost in books, but not on computer screens. Given this distinction, it is feasible to break sentences that carry onto multiple lines differently on screens than on paper.

Consider the two texts displayed in Figure 5-9. The text at the top is packed, or blocked, with the maximum number of words per line (given a line length of 60 characters). The text at the bottom is broken at natural phrasing points. Breaks of this type make the text far easier to read, especially for poor readers (Bork, 1982). Note that the severely ragged right margin does not present eye movement problems, although a severely ragged left margin definitely would. In addition, note that it would be ridiculous to try to doubly justify text when formatted in this manner because the variations in line lengths are too large.

While good readers can generally cope with a wide range of text formats (including very coarse justification), poor readers benefit greatly from techniques such as those just described. Intelligent text formatting helps poor readers ride the text's ebb and flow and infer meaning from

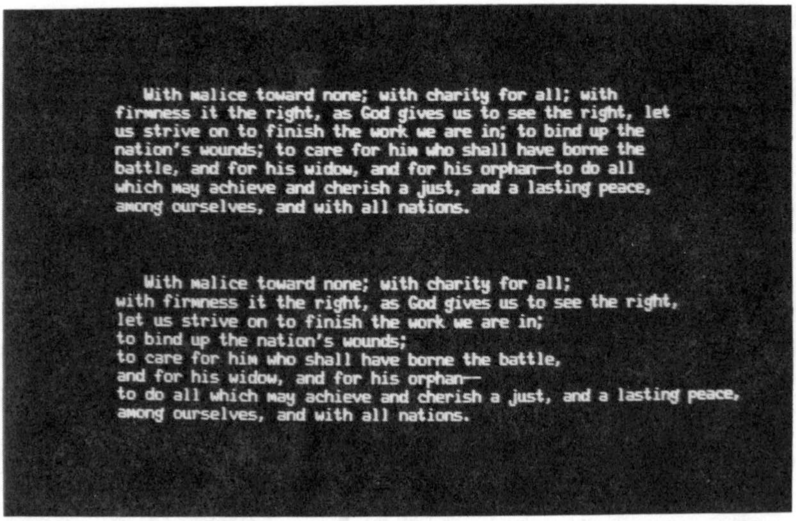

FIGURE 5-9.   *Random Line Breaks vs. Breaks at Natural Phrasing Points.*

otherwise opaque passages. Remember, however, that no display technique is a substitute for clear, effective writing.

Character Attributes

Attributes are optional qualities of graphics entities that change their appearance. A number of attributes have already been discussed and demonstrated, such as boldface and reverse video. This section introduces a broad range of attributes that can be assigned to text characters and discusses their uses and abuses.

The actual set of attributes supported by your system is probably a subset of those discussed below. Some attributes can be imitated if they are not available as primitives, but this might require some rather tricky programming. Some of these attributes can also be assigned to graphics entities such as lines and blocks as well as to characters, especially if those entities are drawn using a graphics character set. This use can provide a number of interesting effects. The main purpose of character attributes, however, is to lend emphasis to titles and keywords in text. Basic character attributes include type style, boldface, reverse video, and underlining. Other character attributes, available on some systems, include varied text size, text rotation, and color.

Basic Attributes

A character's most distinguishing feature is its *font,* or *type style.* This feature is not really an attribute, because it establishes the overall appearance of the character rather than just embellishing on it. Type styles are critical to discussions of character attributes, however, because they generally determine which attributes will "look good" when assigned to various characters. If it is not possible to define your own character sets, the font available on your system is probably firmly fixed. You will find, however, that this font influences your choice of attributes to use for emphasizing text.

The *boldface* and *reverse video* attributes have already been discussed at length, but it is worthwhile here to draw your attention to two design guidelines involving these attributes. The first guideline has been mentioned previously: it is advisable to leave an extra reverse video space before and after any word displayed in reverse video. This assures that each pixel in the first and last characters is surrounded by reverse video pixels. Without these extra spaces, character strokes bordering on the edges of the character cells can be lost as they blend into the screen background (see Figure 5-10).

The second guideline involves the assignment of multiple attributes to a single character: reverse video on low-quality monitors often looks

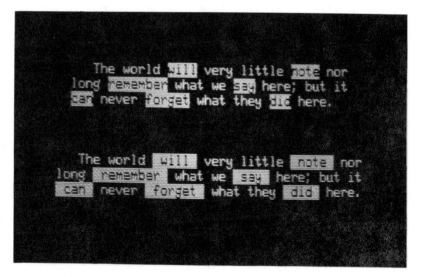

FIGURE 5-10. *Reverse Video With and Without Extra Spaces.*

poor, but can sometimes be improved by assigning *both* the reverse video and boldface attributes simultaneously. Although the above statement is qualified and is not a very strong claim, this guideline teaches two important lessons:

1. Do not overlook the possibility of assigning multiple character attributes to achieve the effects you desire.
2. Be aware that the same attributes can look very dissimilar on systems with different TV monitors, even though the computer component is the same.

Underlining is one character attribute that can usually be simulated (on bit-mapped systems) if it is not available as a primitive. All you have to do is draw a line under the text. This is perhaps the easiest of all attributes to use and has the most consistent visual effect from one system to another. It is useful for emphasizing titles, but its use in lines of text can be distracting if it interferes with the readability of the next lower line. I have found that increased text size is a more pleasing way to emphasize titles, and italics (when available) have fewer side effects in lines of text. (These attributes are discussed later.)

Blinking and *flashing* are probably the strongest visual attributes you can add to text because they immediately catch the student's eye. The terms "blinking" and "flashing" are generally used as synonyms to refer to the intermittent display of a graphics entity. These are two distinct ways in which these attributes can be implemented, one in which the text actually appears and disappears in an on and off manner, and the other in which the text alternates between normal and boldface display but is always visible on the screen. It would be wrong, however, to call one of these implementations blinking and the other flashing, because these labels are not applied consistently in the literature. It is therefore best to use whichever term is used in your system's manual.

Blinking and flashing should be used sparingly. In addition, you should never blink or flash two separate areas of the screen at the same time, because the drawing power of the two will create detrimental competition for the student's attention. Blinking and flashing can often be combined with boldface and reverse video to create more subtle and varied effects. You must experiment with your own computer/video system to see just how they interact and whether the resultant effects are pleasing.

Size of Text

Some systems provide no capability whatever to vary text size. Others provide almost infinite variation, and still others fall somewhere in between. This section discusses several different ways to vary text sizes, from the simplest to the most sophisticated.

The most elementary techniques for varying text size are usually found on systems with only character cell level addressing. These systems typically provide one or two alternate text sizes, such as double width or double height. Figure 5-11 shows the standard, double width, and double height sizes on an industrial standard screen. Note that the double height attribute on this system is actually double width as well. That is, both the double width and double height attributes reduce the number of available character spaces per line on this screen from 80 to 40. As you will see in the discussion that follows, more sophisticated systems uncouple the height and width controls so that you can have tall, narrow characters as well as short, wide ones.

The next level of sophistication and all subsequent ones require a bit-mapped system. At this level, the system provides a large number of standard text sizes as shown in Figure 5-12. In the system pictured, the larger text sizes are achieved by employing a *pixel multiplier*. This means

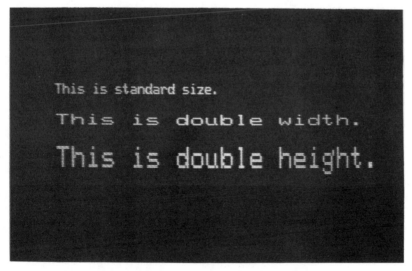

FIGURE 5-11. *Typical Text Sizes on a Character Cell System.*

FIGURE 5-12. *Typical Text Sizes on a Bit-Mapped System.*

that the character's bit pattern is defined by its basic bit map, no matter what its size. If you wish to display the character in Size 2, you simply turn on four dots for each bit in the bit pattern. For Size 3, you turn on 9 dots, and so on. (This is somewhat oversimplified, but the concept is correct.)

As shown in Figure 5-12, the pixel multiplier sizing technique yields block-type characters which often exhibit severe staircasing. The PLATO system has a somewhat different technique for displaying large characters: it lengthens each character stroke into a line rather than multiplying the pixels. This technique yields smoother letters than a pixel multiplier (see Figure 5-13), but displays characters more slowly. Each line must be drawn individually rather than using the fast bit-map-to-dot hardware (discussed in Chapter 1) that is built into most video systems. The PLATO technique also yields characters with thin lines as opposed to the thick lines of a pixel multiplier system. Neither system can be said to be better; it is a matter of taste.

One interesting effect that can be achieved with the PLATO technique involves repeatedly writing a character in a large size, offset slightly each time. This can yield a somewhat three-dimensional graphic as shown in Figure 5-14. Another offshoot of PLATO's character sizing technique is that it allows characters of any size. That is, one can specify Size 2 or Size 5 characters, or Size 2.7 or Size 4.1 characters. The

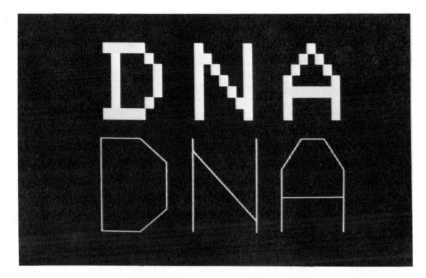

FIGURE 5-13. *Large Text in Block and Line Styles.*

FIGURE 5-14. *Special Effects With Large, Line Style Text on PLATO.*

lengths of the character strokes are computed directly from the command argument and the characters are drawn approrpiately (within the limitations of the screen's resolution).

The most sophisticated systems in regard to text size are those that allow you to control character height and width independently. Some of the effects that can be achieved with this type of system are shown in Figure 5-15. This amount of latitude lets screen designers control the "feel" of their text as well as its size.

Text size, like other character attributes, should not be used haphazardly. It is best to choose one size for the main body of your text and stick to it. You can then use other sizes for titles, emphasis, and special effects without confusing your students.

Rotation

Text rotation has three distinct forms:

- writing line rotation,
- letter rotation, and
- italicization.

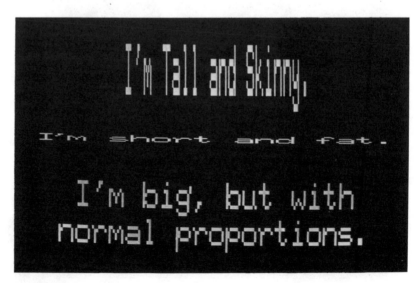

FIGURE 5-15. *Independent Control of Character Height and Width.*

Writing line rotation can be used to a limited degree on systems with only character cell level addressing, but letter rotation and italicization require bit-mapped systems. These three forms of rotation can be used alone or in combination to emphasize text or to produce unusual effects.

Writing line rotation denotes changing the direction of the base line on which letters are written. Figure 5-16 shows the types of writing line rotation that can be achieved on a character cell level system, while Figure 5-17 shows what can be done on a bit-mapped system. Note that in each case the orientation of each individual letter is straight up and down. The letters are displayed normally; only the base line on which they are written is changed. The added addressing capabilities of bit-mapped systems do not change the basic nature, but they make it possible to set the writing line at a greater number of angles.

On bit-mapped systems, writing line rotation is often combined with *letter rotation*. Letter rotation is achieved by rotating the *entire* character cell *without distorting* its basic rectangular shape (see Figure 5-18). The fact that the basic shape of the character cell remains rectangular is the major difference between letter rotation and italicization. When letter rotation is combined with writing line rotation, effects such as those in Figure 5-19 can be achieved.

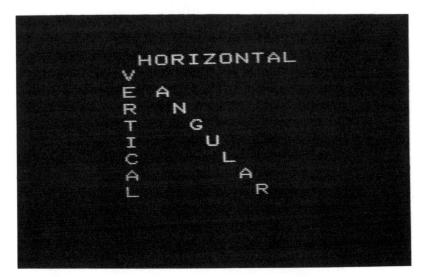

FIGURE 5-16. *Writing Line Rotation on a Character Cell System.*

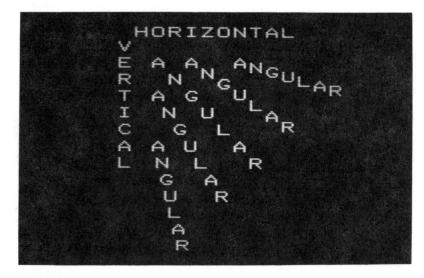

FIGURE 5-17. *Writing Line Rotation on a Bit-Mapped System.*

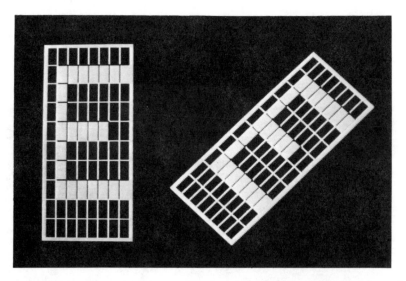

FIGURE 5-18. *Letter Rotation. Note that the basic shape of the character cell is* not *distorted.*

Italicization is distortion of the basic shape of the character cells to produce slanted or tilted text (see Figure 5-20). The character cell for an italicized letter is no longer a rectangle, but a parallelogram. It is as

FIGURE 5-19. *Combined Letter and Writing Line Rotation.*

FIGURE 5-20. *Italicization. Note the distortion in the basic shape of the character cell.*

if the top of the letter had been pushed over while the bottom remained fixed. Note carefully that the top and bottom boundaries of the character remain horizontal. This feature distinguishes italicization from letter rotation, as shown in Figure 5-21.

FIGURE 5-21. *Straight vs. Rotated vs. Italicized Text.*

Each system has a different optimum italicization angle which depends on the number of pixels in its character cell. The optimum angle is the one that exhibits the least amount of staircasing. Some systems provide only one italicization angle (set to the optimum), while others literally draw italicized characters and therefore allow any angle to be used. With the latter systems, it is best to experiment to find the optimum angle and then stick to it. Staircased letters will surely "look funny" to your students and detract from readability.

When available, italicization is an excellent technique for emphasizing keywords in text (see Figures 2-1, 2-3, 2-5, and 4-10). It is distinctive, yet subtle. It attracts readers' attention without causing severe breaks in their reading rhythm. For these reasons you will see italicization used widely in books. Indeed, you may have noticed that typeset materials very seldom use underlining. This is one instance in which a visual effect in printed materials is virtually identical to its effect on computer screens. Therefore, the use of italics is highly recommended.

Color

Color is as effective for highlighting text as it is for highlighting any other graphics entity. When it is used, two basic qualities should be considered:

1. Make sure that adjacent colors complement each other (that they don't clash).
2. Don't use colors that are too "hot."

Both of these guidelines are intended to avoid the same problem caused by blinking and flashing: catching the reader's eye so strongly that reading rhythm is disturbed and readability suffers.

Clashing colors are often difficult to avoid if you don't know how well your students' monitors (computer screens) have been adjusted. That is, a nice Kelly green on your monitor may come out as a muddy olive green on another monitor. But if the monitors are reasonably adjusted, you will probably find that color combinations such as red and yellow or blue and green are not desirable. Video systems differ considerably in color *hue* (shade) and *saturation* (brightness), so "blue" on a perfectly adjusted Apple is usually different from "blue" on a perfectly adjusted Texas Instrument computer. In addition, the standard rules for combining colors on paper may not apply to your screen because paper is reflective while computer screens are luminous. You will have to experiment with the colors on your system to discover which are most complementary.

All systems tend to have one or two "hot" colors like pink or magenta. These colors are referred to as "hot" because they may actually appear to pulsate on the screen. Such colors may be good for some graphics applications, but they are seldom satisfactory for text display and should be avoided.

The question as to what color to choose for your basic text still remains. The answer lies in the way color is produced on TV screens. Most TVs create colors by mixing red, green, and blue phosphors in varying intensities. White is produced by mixing all three colors in their maximum intensities. This technique is fine when the TV is viewed from an armchair across the room, but it can be very tiring on the eyes if the TV is viewed from close by and if the three electron guns that excite the screen phosphors are not perfectly adjusted.

To display any one of the three primary colors (red, green, and blue), TVs need to use only one of their three electron guns. These colors are therefore referred to as *monochromatic,* and display of any one of them individually is usually much sharper than display of any color requiring their combination. For this reason, you should choose one of the primary colors as your main text color. I recommend using either green or blue, because these are generally softer than red. Displaying your text in a monochromatic color will get the most out of

whatever monitor you use and be easiest for your students to view for
extended periods.

Use vs. Overuse

All screen design techniques are vulnerable to overuse, but character
attributes are perhaps the most vulnerable because they are the easiest
to abuse. For example, one of the first programs that many people write
on color graphics systems is a routine to display their names in large
letters with each letter in a different color. This is fine for demonstrating
the terminal's capabilities, but it would be a poor technique to use on
a screen that you expect students to read.

Subtle uses of character attributes are recommended:

- Use blinking or flashing only for very important messages and
  never in two screen locations at the same time.
- Use italicization if possible to emphasize text without decreasing
  readability.
- Stick to a single size for most text.
- Avoid "hot" colors.

These guidelines speak more for restraint than for splash. The overall
governing factor in any screen design is the subject matter itself. If your
design techniques upstage the subject matter, they may be visually interesting, but they will not be instructionally effective.

Writing Modes

If you try to display a letter in a character cell that already contains
another letter, the new letter usually *replaces* the old one (see Figure 5-
22). This result occurs because both the 0 bits and the 1 bits in the
character bit map cause actions to occur. (Refer to Figure 3-9 if you
need to review character bit maps.) It is easy to think of the 1 bits as
turning dots on, but don't forget that the 0 bits can also turn dots off.
Thus, printing a line of Xs on top of a line of 0s usually results in a line
of Xs, not a line of ⊠s. *Usually*, that is, but not *always*.

The video system's behavior when two letters are displayed in the
same character cell is dependent upon its *writing mode*. If the system

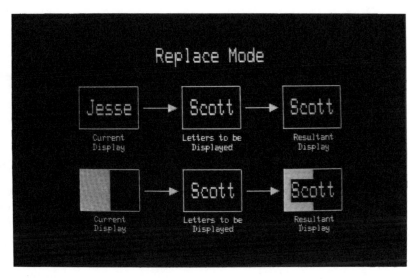

FIGURE 5-22. *Writing in Replace Mode.*

behaves in the manner described above, it is said to be in *replace mode*. This is the only writing mode available on many character cell level systems, and it is the default, or basic, mode on most bit-mapped systems. On some systems, however, one or more additional modes are available: *erase, overlay,* and *complement*.

These four writing modes do not reflect precisely any particular computer/video system; therefore the following discussion is representative rather than based on a specific system. Different systems have different combinations of these modes, refer to them by different names, and even sometimes handle special cases in slightly different ways. For example, the default writing mode on PLATO is overlay rather than replace, and the PLATO literature refers to these two modes as "write" and "rewrite," respectively. In addition, PLATO does not have a complement writing mode. Refer to your system's manuals for the exact writing modes available on your system.

In some respects, erase, overlay, and complement modes are actually easier to understand than replace mode, because the 0 bits in these three modes are generally *passive*. This means that in all writing modes except replace mode, you have to worry only about how the 1 bits are reproduced. When writing in normal video, the 0 bits neither turn on nor turn off dots, but simply act as place holders in the bit map.

You may be surprised that reverse video is not considered a writing mode. The reason is that reverse video, like all other character attributes, can be combined with each of the four writing modes to produce special effects, while the writing modes themselves are mutually exclusive. That is, the system can be in only one writing mode at a time, but you can assign a number of character attributes simultaneously. Writing modes determine the basic actions that the video system takes for each bit in the character bit map. Character attributes determine the additional visual effects that embellish those basic actions. Consider, for example, what happens if the system is in replace mode and you try to display a letter on top of another letter. The letter underneath is always replaced, regardless of whether the new letter is in normal or reverse video. All reverse video actually does is switch contexts: it treats all 1 bits as if they were 0s and all 0 bits as if they were 1s.

With these important concepts in mind, consider the effects of *erase mode*. In this mode, the 1 bits turn dots off. (Don't forget that the 0 bits do nothing. If they turned dots on, erase mode would be identical to replace mode with the reverse video attribute. But it isn't!) If you display text in erase mode on a blank screen, nothing appears. But if you display text in erase mode on top of other graphics entities, the dots corresponding to 1 bits in the character bit map are turned off (see Figure 5-23). This mode is useful for labeling colored or shaded areas

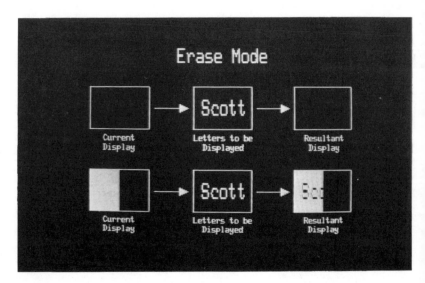

FIGURE 5-23. *Writing in Erase Mode.*

as shown in Figure 5-24. It is also useful for wipe erases as described in Chapter 2.

Overlay mode is like replace mode in that the 1 bits turn dots on, but it differs from replace mode because the 0 bits are passive and do not turn dots off (see Figure 5-25). Thus it is possible in overlay mode

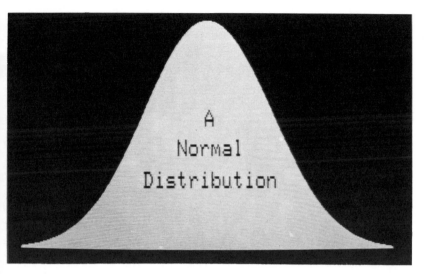

FIGURE 5-24.   *Sample Use of Text in Erase Mode.*

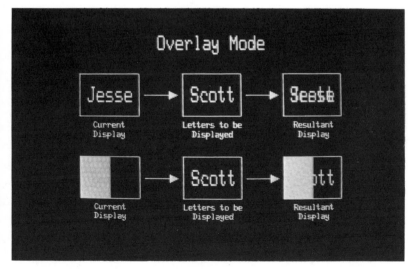

FIGURE 5-25.   *Writing in Overlay Mode.*

to display a line of Xs on top of a line of 0s and come up with a line of ⊗s. One of the valuable uses of this mode is to squeeze letters together in special situations. For example, Figure 5-26 shows several lines of text spaced closer together vertically than normal. In replace mode, parts of the upper lines are erased when the lower lines are written because the 0 bits turn dots off. In overlay mode, all of the lines are readable. Squeezing text in this manner is not recommended for general practice, but it can get you out of a jam in certain situations.

The most complex writing mode is *complement mode,* because the action taken by the 1 bits depends on the current state of the corresponding dot on the screen. If the dot is currently off, the 1 bit turns it on. But if the dot is currently on, the 1 bit turns it off (see Figure 5-27). Thus the 1 bits in the character bit map cause the corresponding dots to be changed to their complementary states. As shown in Figure 5-28, complement mode is valuable for labels that span both shaded and open areas.

Text as a Graphics Entity

Character attributes and writing modes make text on computer/video systems more than just a verbal communication tool: they allow it to

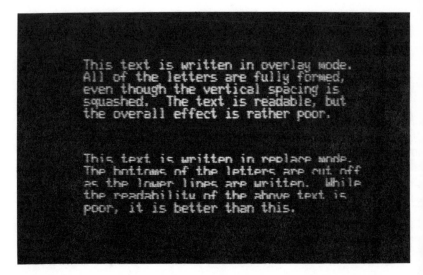

FIGURE 5-26. *Squeezing Text Vertically in Overlay and Replace Modes.*

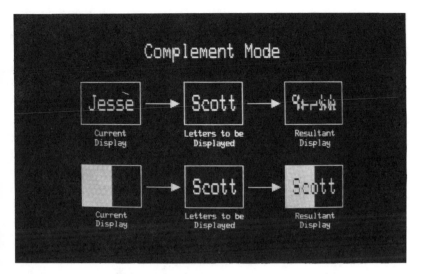

FIGURE 5-27. *Writing in Complement Mode.*

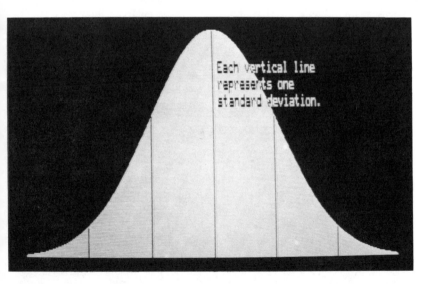

FIGURE 5-28. *Sample Use of Text in Complement Mode.*

be a visual communication tool as well. In addition to all of the visual effects discussed in this chapter, two other text display dimensions remain: *timing* and *animation*.

As discussed at the end of Chapter 2, Alfred Bork (1982) likes to display text at a rate slow enough for students to read it as it comes up on the screen. Given this approach, Bork is able to add emphasis to keywords in his materials by adding pauses at appropriate points. Thus timing itself becomes a display characteristic in Bork's materials, and text display takes on a fluid characteristic that mimics certain graphics techniques in film and television.

Text can also be animated on the screen in the same manner as the stagecoach for "How the West Was One + Three × Four," discussed in Chapter 3. It is usually much easier to animate blocks of characters than pictures, because the time needed for the computer/video system to draw the pictures often destroys any feeling of motion. Text animation can be used very effectively in a large number of applications.

Consider, for example, the graphic in Figure 5-29, which was used to explain the concept of reading a file from a disk to prepare it for editing it in the computer's main memory. This diagram was drawn on a character cell level system with a graphics character set. To illustrate the file's moving from the disk into the computer's main memory, the words "File 2" were animated across the screen from left to right. The multiple images in Figure 5-30 give you some of the feel for this effect.

These two techniques are prime examples of how text can come alive on video screens and need not be simply a reproduction of its

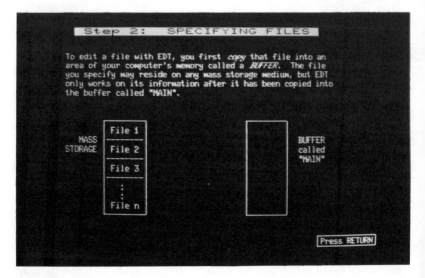

FIGURE 5-29. *A Display Set Up for Text Animation.*

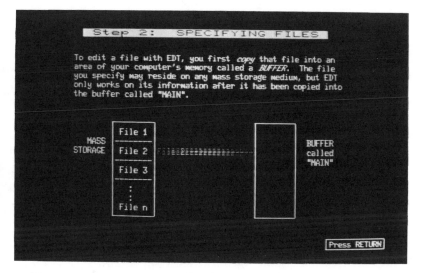

FIGURE 5-30.   *Effect of Animating Text.*

counterpart in printed media. A word of warning: while you are exploring and using all the techniques at your disposal, be alert to guard against their overuse. Limited and tasteful use of visual enhancements when displaying text can clarify points for your students and help maintain their interest.

Chapter Summary

Text continues to be a major channel through which computers communicate messages to students, especially messages that tell students what they should do next. Above all, these messages must be clear and well written. While graphics and symbols can be used to clarify and punctuate messages' meanings, no screen design techniques can substitute for good, basic writing.

Readability on computer/video systems is different from readability in printed materials due to several inherent differences between the two media. In general, the readability of a given text passage on a video screen is poorer than it would be in print. Text displays should therefore be formatted with careful consideration of type style, line length, justification, and break points. Type style should be kept simple, with short lines broken at natural phrases. Text should be justified at one margin only, preferably the left.

A number of different attributes can sometimes be applied to text characters. These include boldface, reverse video, underlining, blinking or flashing, size, rotation, and color. These attributes are valuable for adding emphasis to text, but they should be used with restraint. Overuse can seriously impair readability in addition to having a detrimental effect on the screen's visual appeal.

Some computer/video systems provide a number of different writing modes that alter the translation of a character bit map into screen dots in some basic way. For example, erase mode turns dots corresponding to 1 bits off rather than on, while overlay mode inhibits erasing of dots corresponding to 0 bits. The names and actions of these modes vary somewhat from system to system, but their basic functionalities are typically a subset of the four described here.

Text on computer/video systems can be used as a graphics entity as well as a medium for displaying words. For example, it can be displayed at various speeds, using pauses to add emphasis to keywords. In addition, words and short phrases can often be effectively animated across the screen to denote a flow of information and/or materials. These techniques are especially useful for computer-naive audiences.

Issues and Activities

1. How important is text in your CAI materials? Is it a major source of information for your students or are most messages conveyed in some other way?

2. Which of the following text attributes exist on your system? What are the instructions you must program or the special characters you must print to display text with these attributes?
   • blinking or flashing
   • boldface
   • color
   • italicization
   • multiple fonts
   • reverse video

- rotation
- underlining
- various character sizes

3. Which of the following writing modes exist on your system? What are the instructions you must program or the special characters you must print to display text in these modes?
   - complement
   - erase
   - overlay
   - replace

4. If you have access to more than one type of computer/video system, compare the visual qualities of various text attributes on the different systems. Do some systems seem to be optimized for certain attributes?

5. Review a number of CAI programs and evaluate the clarity of their text messages. How would you use the techniques discussed in this chapter to improve the quality of communication in these programs?

6. The desirability of using various text attributes to highlight text depends as much on personal taste as it does on your system's display capabilities. Experiment with the attributes on your system to identify which you like best in different situations. Compare your assessments with those of a colleague.

7. Text sizes have distinctive characteristics, regardless of whether they are block or line style. As the height-to-width ratio changes (see Figure 5-15), the "feel" of the text can also change significantly. Experiment with the text size commands on your system to determine which are most suitable for normal text, which for titles, and which for highlighted messages.

8. The four writing modes discussed in this chapter are seldom, if ever, all available on one system with the exact functionality described. On a large variety of systems, however, the missing modes can often be simulated. For example, the erase mode demonstration at the bottom of Figure 5-23 was simulated on my system by writing "Scott" first in overlay mode and then rewriting it in complement mode. Try to implement all four writing modes on your system, simulating those that are not available as primitives. Talk to an experienced programmer if you need assistance.

9. Implement text animation on your system with a display similar to that in Figure 5-30. When would this technique be useful in CAI courses for your major subject matter area?

10. The qualities of text rotation and italicization depend largely on the angles chosen. Determine the rotation and italicization angles on your own system that exhibit the least amount of staircasing.

·6·

Screen Design Tools

The orientation throughout this book has been on how computer screens appear to students. Relatively little has been said about how you actually get computers to display text and graphics according to your specifications. I firmly believe that design is a far more difficult skill to master than programming, and I continually encourage educators to concentrate on design and leave programming to people who thrive on it. There are usually hordes of exuberant student programmers in every high school and college who would jump at the chance to program a "real" application that will be used by other students. In addition, these programmers can often contribute considerable insight into how your materials will work with the intended target population. Materials produced using an educator/programmer team are often educationally sounder and visually more creative than materials produced by either an educator or a programmer alone.

It is impossible, however, to take full advantage of the computer/video medium without hands-on experience and an understanding of basic computer/video functions. For example, while selection of functional areas should be made mostly on pedagogical grounds, knowledge of erase primitives can allow you to plan for pop and wipe erases rather than having to settle for the slow, tedious technique of printing a space into each character cell. But saying you should interact with the computer to gain basic knowledge of its capabilities and a feel for its various visual effects is not the same as saying you should become a programmer. Programming is a very worthwhile skill to develop in its own right, and you should definitely learn how to write simple computer programs during the course of your studies. However, there are a number of *screen design tools* that bridge the gap between ideas and implementation, and, in the long run, familiarity with these tools will probably pay higher dividends than will programming skills.

Screen design tools can play a number of roles, from simply helping you visualize screen layouts to automatically generating the computer code necessary to reproduce your design from inside a CAI program. This chapter considers a number of tools that span this continuum. It begins by taking a look at general issues that relate to the implementation of screen designs, focusing on the designer's perspective and techniques that can be used to simplify design implementation. It then examines software tools that can act as sketchpads for screen design and hardware and software tools that can provide assistance in generating the computer code necessary to reproduce specific screen designs. The last two sections discuss how screen design tools can be interfaced with CAI programs and take a look at the nature of courseware transportability and its implications for screen design.

The Designer's Working Level

Imagine that you want to add a room to your house.[1] Certainly with a project of this scope you can't just go out and start buying lumber. You begin by making a plan, usually in the form of a rough sketch on paper. This sketch helps you visualize your plan and determine general proportions. In most instances, this first plan is drawn freehand, does not include measurements, and concentrates on major features rather than exact details. The plan certainly is not made with wood, nails, and concrete footings.

When designing computer screens, you must likewise be able to separate yourself from programming and other implementation issues that relate to generating the computer code necessary to display your design. If you do not, two things happen:

- you quickly lose sight of your overall design and become entangled in programming details, and

---

1. The author is indebted to Peter Dean for his guidance toward development of the ideas in this section.

• you invest so much time in developing a single design that you are loath to make any changes if the design proves faulty.

These problems are caused by working at too low a level. You must be able to design quickly, while ideas are hot, capturing the layout for an entire course or module at one sitting. Your initial design must be created inexpensively in a fluid medium so it can be changed readily and easily when faults show up—as they always do—in designs for individual lessons or displays.

Luckily, most computer/video systems have a number of tools that lend themselves directly to the development of screen design sketchpads. Such sketchpads allow you to concentrate on the highest level of screen design: how displays will look to your students. They mask programming issues until your designs are ready for incorporating into lessons. At that point you might have to give a copy of your design to a programmer, or you might be able to issue a command to generate the computer codes necessary to reproduce it from within a CAI program. The precise nature of the task is dependent upon the tool.

In addition to letting you work at the highest level of screen design, most tools also make it possible for you to separate *lesson logic,* the instructions that perform behind-the-scenes tasks such as answer-judging, from *display logic,* the instructions that generate visual images students see on the screen. The advantages of this separation cannot be overstated:

1. The separation allows you to correct simple display problems like typographical errors without having to edit the program code (which can introduce more serious errors).
2. The separation simplifies debugging by isolating the two components and making each smaller and easier to work with.
3. The separation reduces the amount of information that must be stored in the computer's memory as the program is running (by allowing displays to be stored in disk files), making it easier to fit complex programs on small systems.
4. The separation enhances the *transportability* of CAI programs from one system to another by isolating that part of the program that is usually unique to each system (the display logic).

In some situations, any one of these advantages is enough to justify the use of screen design tools. Getting all four in the same bargain is usually enough to convince all but the most stubborn do-it-yourself courseware developers.

Text Editors

A large number of powerful text editors are now available for virtually all computer/video systems, especially those targeted toward business markets. Most of these editors have evolved to satisfy the needs of people using computers for word processing. To be useful for CAI screen design, a text editor needs only two essential qualities: it must allow you to move the cursor anywhere on the screen, and it must then allow you to insert or delete characters at that point. Editors with these qualities are referred to as *screen-oriented* as opposed to *line-oriented* or *character-oriented* editors which require that you replot your entire screen to see the results of your editing commands in context. The editor in most BASIC language environments, for example, is a line-oriented editor.

Screen-oriented text editors can be used to design graphics entities as well as text passages, even if your CAI course will ultimately be displayed on a bit-mapped screen. The reason for this relates directly to working levels. The previous section stated that initial designs should be done quickly and inexpensively, capturing ideas while they're hot without investing a level of effort that later discourages changes. Given these premises, many graphics entities can simply be noted or approximated in character cell level graphics so that you do not spend a lot of time worrying about each individual pixel on your first pass.

For example, Figures 6-1 and 6-2 show the initial and final drafts of the same figure. Figure 6-1 was created in several minutes using a screen-oriented text editor. Figure 6-2 was created by writing a short program to call a sequence of bit map graphics primitives. Certainly, the latter figure is a better representation of the author's original idea, but its production took considerably more computer knowledge and substantially more time. (The meaning of these figures is explained in Chapter 7.)

Text Blocks and Text Ports

The best use of screen-oriented text editors, of course, is for laying out text. This is what these tools are designed to do, and they generally possess a number of qualities that facilitate the process.

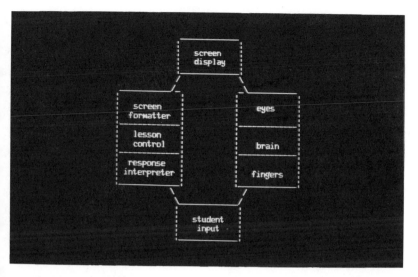

FIGURE 6-1.   *A Diagram Created Using a Screen-Oriented Text Editor.*

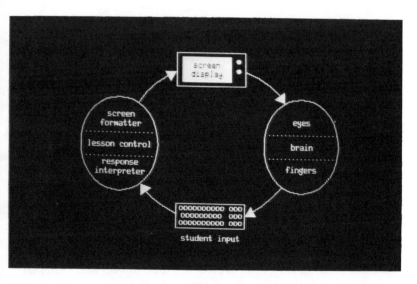

FIGURE 6-2.   *A Diagram Created by Calling Bit Map Graphics Primitives.*

The first such quality is the ability to see precisely how a text message will look on students' screens. You can see immediately if a message is too wordy, whether it will fit in a predefined functional area, and where lines should be broken to emphasize natural phrasing. Once you have typed the message into the editor, you can usually move it around on the screen, change line lengths, and otherwise reformat the text without having to retype it. When the display is satisfactory, you can save it for future use. This does not *necessarily* mean that you will be able to regenerate the stored display *from within a CAI program.* It simply means that the screen can be regenerated *by the text editor.* The implications of different storage techniques for interfacing with CAI programs are discussed later.

Screen-oriented text editors have different levels of sophistication. In their simplest mode, these editors allow you to move the cursor around the screen and insert or delete characters at any point. At the other end of the spectrum, some editors allow you to specify margins within which text is to be displayed and will automatically format your message within these margins as you type. Editors of the former variety are said to support *text blocks,* while those of the latter variety are said to support *text ports.*

Suppose, for example, that you wish to display the first part of Lincoln's Gettysburg Address in the format shown in Figure 6-3. With a text block editor, you move the cursor to wherever you want the first "F" and type the first line. After you type the comma, you press the RETURN key. This action positions the cursor on the next line, either just below the first "F" or at the extreme left-hand margin of the screen,

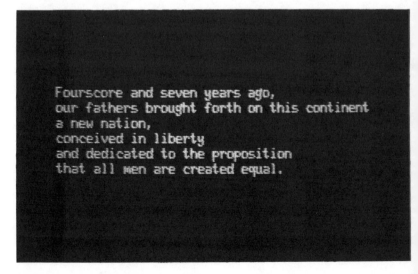

FIGURE 6-3. *A Text Passage With Controlled Line Breaks Created Using a Text Block Editor.*

depending upon your editor's functionality. If the former action occurs, you are ready to begin typing the second line, but in the latter case you must first space or tab over to the correct column. You then continue by typing each line and pressing RETURN at the end of each, until all six lines are displayed.

The functionality of a text port editor is somewhat different. You begin by telling the system the left and right margin positions, or perhaps the margin position and the line length. You then position the cursor and start typing, but you do not press RETURN at the end of each line. You simply keep typing. The editor automatically detects when a word has gone past the right-hand margin and inserts one or more line terminators (often a carriage return/line feed pair) to position the surplus word on the next line at the specified left-hand margin. Figure 6-4 shows the result of this technique with screen column 20 defined as the left margin position and a line length of 43 characters.

It is considerably faster to enter text via text ports than via text blocks. Unfortunately, the text in Figure 6-4 isn't in the desired format shown in Figure 6-3. This is easily corrected by moving the cursor to the first letter of each word that should begin a new line and pressing RETURN. The two results are then identical.

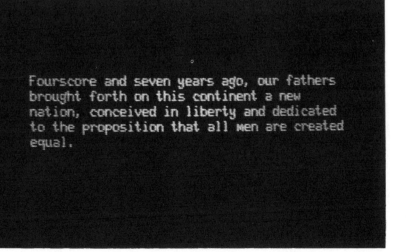

FIGURE 6-4.   *A Text Passage With Uncontrolled Line Breaks Created Using a Text Port Editor.*

The real difference between text blocks and text ports shows itself when you return to a piece of text to edit or reformat it. Assume that you begin with the text display shown at the top of Figure 6-5 and wish to reformat it to achieve the display at the bottom of Figure 6-5. With a text block editor, you have to do considerable work moving the cursor, deleting line terminators, adding or deleting extra spaces, repositioning the cursor, and putting in new line terminators. With a text port editor, you only need to specify new values for the margins and the text is reformatted automatically. The same situation applies if you decide to add new text between two existing text passages (see Figure 6-6). Text block editors require extensive reformatting, while text port editors readjust line breaks automatically.

The decision of whether to use text blocks or text ports depends on your editor's capabilities, the type of text you intend to display, and your own taste. Both editors, however, allow you to manipulate text displays visually so that you can see how your screen designs will actually look and refine them accordingly. These capabilities are much more difficult to achieve if you rely on PRINT or WRITE statements in a computer language to format your text.

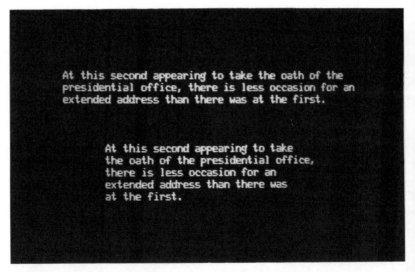

FIGURE 6-5. *Text Reformatting Caused by Margin Adjustments.*

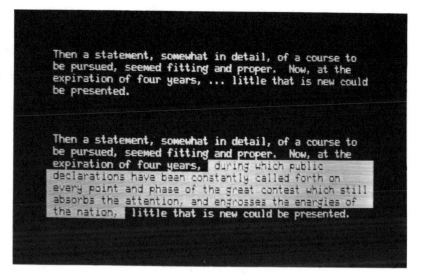

Then a statement, somewhat in detail, of a course to
be pursued, seemed fitting and proper. Now, at the
expiration of four years, ... little that is new could
be presented.

Then a statement, somewhat in detail, of a course to
be pursued, seemed fitting and proper. Now, at the
expiration of four years, during which public
declarations have been constantly called forth on
every point and phase of the great contest which still
absorbs the attention, and engrosses the energies of
the nation, little that is new could be presented.

FIGURE 6-6. *Text Reformatting Caused by Insertion of New Text.*

Graphics Editors

Graphics editors allow graphics entities to be created and manipulated
in many of the same ways that screen-oriented text editors provide for
text. Due to the increased complexity of graphics, however, graphics
editors are usually considerably more complicated. For example, they
often make it possible to change the size and rotation angle of pictures
as well as text, in addition to moving them around on the screen. Most
graphics editors also make it possible to assign attributes to characters
and graphics entities, while this is usually beyond the capabilities of most
text editors.

Graphics editors vary greatly in their capabilities and modes of operation, even in some basic functions. These differences are often attrib-
utable to special characteristics of the computer/video system for which
an editor was designed. But you do not have to use most of a graphics
editor's esoteric functions when you are drafting initial screen designs.
As stated earlier, the real power of using editors in any capacity during

the design stage is the ability to store trial designs and come back to fill in or change details at a later time. You might therefore put a simple box on the screen to indicate where a more complex figure will be inserted later. As your design evolves, you might change the size and position of this box several times—very quick and easy operations with many graphics editors—and wait to add the actual figure until the screen layout is frozen.

Of course, the main advantages of working with graphics editors become visible only when you begin designing graphics entities. Graphics editors make it possible to draw figures and pictures without worrying about the esoteric computer code necessary to generate such pictures. Editors also raise the screen designer's working level to a point that enables him or her to concentrate on overall visual effect rather than the intricate details of code implementation. Knowledge of computer graphics code will help you understand how to use some special graphics techniques and help you convey your intentions to programmers, but your knowledge of effective screen design will reap greater profits for your students.

Graphics editors can save a lot of time if you wish to incorporate complex figures into your CAI programs. Consider, for example, a lesson that incorporates a map like that shown in Figure 6-7. There are

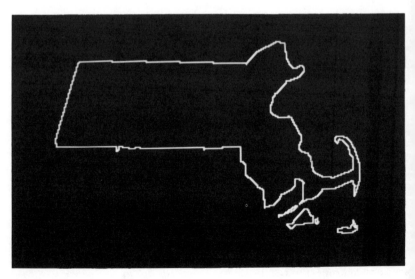

FIGURE 6-7. *A Complex Figure to Be Stored on the Computer.*

three basic ways to get the information needed to draw this map into the computer:

1. You can figure out the critical points using a piece of graph paper and enter these into a data file or program by typing at the keyboard.
2. You can make a large transparency of the map, tape it in front of your screen, and trace it using the arrow keys or a light pen while a graphics editor captures your input.
3. You can place a copy of the map on a graphics tablet and trace it with a mouse or other such device while a graphics editor captures your input.

The technique you choose will depend on the hardware and software you have available and the capabilities of your graphics editor. All three of these techniques, however, will allow you to do the job faster than trying to write a map-drawing program from scratch. In addition, the use of a graphics editor will greatly reduce the effort needed to make modifications once the figure is stored on the computer.

Interfacing Tools with CAI Programs

The discussion throughout this chapter may have convinced you that screen design tools can increase courseware development efficiency even if all you can do with their final product is show it to a programmer who will write the required computer code. In most cases, however, these tools do much more. Specifically, they allow you to store the resultant screen in such a way that it can be regenerated from inside a CAI program. Three techniques for accomplishing this task are discussed below:

- storing a copy of the screen's bit map,
- generating executable graphics commands that can be incorporated into your CAI program, and
- storing a callable set of graphics codes or screen primitives.

Storing the Screen's Bit Map

From a conceptual point of view, the easiest way to store a screen image is to copy the internal representation of its bit map from the computer's video memory onto a disk and then copy it back again at a later time. This approach is taken by the Apple BSAVE (binary save) and BLOAD (binary load) commands. This storage procedure literally reads the bit values for every pixel on the screen and stores them in a disk file.

As you would suspect, this process is often very slow. The larger the number of pixels on the screen (that is, the finer the resolution) and the greater the number of bits per pixel (the more attributes each pixel can have), the slower the saving and restoration process. Storing the screen image in this manner also requires a large amount of disk space. An entire Apple diskette, for example can store only 10–12 different screens in this manner. Perhaps the biggest problem with this technique, though, is that it is designed to work on contiguous sections of the screen and cannot be segmented. This means that while the area to be saved can start at any point, in most cases it must extend to the right margin and return all the way to the left margin on the next row of pixels. This technique generally cannot save an area in the center of the screen that does not extend to both margins.

The ability to store the screen's bit map is useful, however, in two special situations. The first such situation involves highly complex screens such as the one shown in Figure 6-8. The commands needed to generate this picture are long and involved, so once the picture is generated it is quicker to store and reload the bit map than to re-execute the commands. The second situation involves screen images that are built up from a number of overlapping displays. In this case, regeneration of the image would require replotting each of the component displays. The visual effect of this action can be rather disconcerting to students as text and graphics are drawn and erased in quick succession. Storing the bit map avoids this problem completely.

Except for these two special situations, storing the bit map is not usually an efficient way to reproduce screen displays. The process takes too long, requires too much disk space, and doesn't allow sufficient control of subsections of the screen. So while devices such as graphics tablets that cater to this storage method are useful for initial stages of screen design, their software controllers must often be modified to allow more efficient storage techniques if the pictures they produce are to be regenerated from within CAI programs.

FIGURE 6-8. *A Complex Display that Can Best Be Stored in Bit Map Form.*

Generating Executable Graphics Commands

A number of screen design tools provide a facility for generating graphics commands that you can incorporate directly into your CAI program. These commands are executable statements in BASIC, Fortran, Pascal, Tutor, LOGO, or some other programming language, and you can insert them into your CAI program at the appropriate point when you want your design displayed.

This technique does not suffer from the inefficiency of storing the screen's entire bit map. Imagine, for example, that you designed a simple graphic like that in Figure 6-9. Instead of storing the entire bit map, you could regenerate this graphic with commands similar to the following: [2]

```
POSITION (0,0)
LINE TO (2,0) (2,2) (0,2) (0,0)
POSITION (1,3)
CIRCLE (1)
POSITION (0,4)
LINE TO (1,6) (2,4) 0,4)
```

2. These commands are not meant to reflect the structure of any particular computer language. They are purely illustrative.

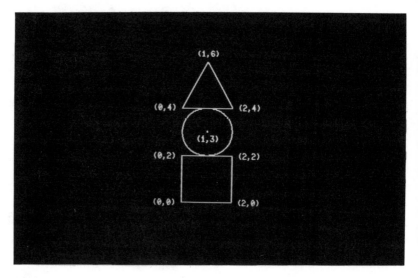

FIGURE 6-9. *A Simple Display that Can Best Be Stored in Graphics Command Form.*

Obviously, the executable commands are a much more efficient representation.

Executable commands do, however, take up space in your CAI program. If you are running on a system with limited memory, this can be a real problem. The best way to get around this problem is to store the graphics representations in disk files that can be *called* by the CAI program when needed. This technique also has the advantage of achieving full display and lesson logic separation as advocated earlier in this chapter.

Storing Callable Graphics Code

Callable graphics code is a set of screen display instructions that can be executed directly from within another program. For example, this code might consist of a set of characters that can be printed on the screen in graphics mode to create special effects. The controlling program usually requires a plotting routine that reads the code from a file, performs any necessary translations and/or transformations, and then passes the commands to the video system which performs the appropriate display functions. This sequence of events is depicted in Figure 6-10. The

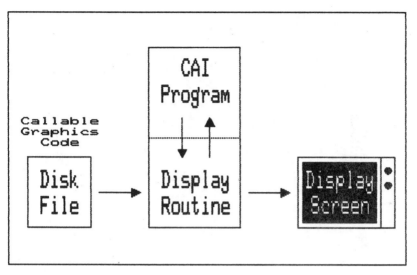

FIGURE 6-10. *Use of Callable Graphics Code by a CAI Program. (After Moreau and Heines, 1980.)*

graphics code is callable because it can be retrieved by the CAI program whenever it is needed and does not take up memory when it is not needed.

In addition to memory conservation, callable graphics codes have a number of other advantages. Consider, for example, the displays in Figure 6-11. If you stored these as either bit maps or executable code, you would probably need a separate representation for each display. Using callable code, however, you could store just the three component shapes and then call them from your CAI program in the appropriate order to generate these (and any other) combinations.

Implications for Courseware Transportability

The major advantage of callable codes, however, really becomes apparent when you consider courseware *transportability*. Transportability refers to the ease with which a program running on one computer/video system can be made to run on another system of a different type. As you are probably aware, the BASIC computer language is available on virtually all microcomputers used in schools. While BASIC is sometimes

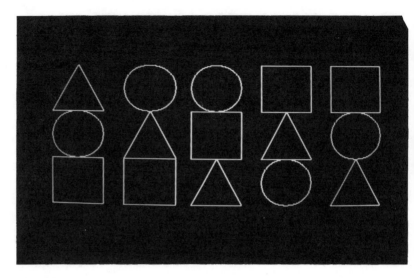

FIGURE 6-11. *Sample Use of Callable Graphics Code.*

criticized when compared to newer programming languages, it is nonetheless the de facto standard for programs intended to run on combinations of the Pets, Apples, TRS-80s, Sinclairs, and other systems that
are so quickly moving into our classrooms.

Interestingly enough, the BASIC languages on these systems are all
very similar, and converting the *lesson* logic from one system to another
is not an overwhelming task. Converting the *display* logic, however, is
a problem of significantly greater magnitude:

- How do you translate bit-mapped graphics into character cell
graphics?
- What can you do if one screen displays 32 rows of 64 columns,
while another displays 24 rows of 80 columns, and still another
displays 20 rows of 40 columns?
- How do you compensate on a less sophisticated system if you're
trying to convert a program that makes heavy use of character
attributes?
- What techniques can you use on black and white systems to make
up for their lack of color?
- What happens when you convert author-defined character sets designed for 7 by 9 character cells to 8 by 10 character cells?

These are only a representative few of many questions with difficult answers. But one thing is certain: if display logic can be isolated from lesson logic, you stand a chance of converting the original program; but if the two types of logic are interwoven you might as well rewrite the program from scratch.

Chapter Summary

A number of tools can be used to simplify the design of computer screens and the translation of those designs into computer code. These tools include screen-oriented text and graphics editors, as well as special hardware and software subsystems (such as graphics tablets) that interface with the two.

One advantage of using such tools is that they raise the designer's working level to a point that permits concentration on the visual effects being designed rather than on the code needed to create those effects. These tools also tend to separate display logic from lesson logic, thus yielding simpler debugging, smaller program size, and easier transportability.

Screen-oriented text editors are generally word processing products, but can be used to approximate graphics as well as text displays. Graphics editors are far more complex and are often tailored for a specific computer/video system. The major advantage of both these editors is that you can draft initial designs quickly, see your designs immediately, and come back to fill in or change details at a later time.

All such tools provide some method for storing screen displays once they are created. Methods for storing screen displays vary, but can usually be classified as storing the screen bit map, generating executable graphics commands, or storing callable graphics code. The first method is the least efficient in terms of time and storage space, while the last is the most efficient. Each method, however, has advantages and disadvantages.

One of the major qualities of screen design tools is that they enhance courseware transportability by separating display logic from lesson logic. Display logic is much more difficult to convert from one computer to another than lesson logic because display logic is much more variable. That is, if you are familiar with one system's form of a specific computer language, you will probably find another system's variety of that same language quite easy to understand. But display commands can be totally different from one system to another due to basic differences in their video components. It is therefore advantageous to separate lesson logic from display logic so that the former can be converted in a straightforward manner while the latter is manipulated to accommodate the characteristics of the new system.

Issues and Activities

1. Find out what screen design tools are available on your system and how to use them. See if you find it easier to build screen displays using these tools or by writing graphics code from scratch.

2. Look at the code for a number of CAI lessons. Is the lesson logic distinct from the display logic, or are the two interwoven?

3. If you have access to a screen-oriented text editor, determine whether it supports text blocks, text ports, or both. How easy is it to reformat text like that shown in Figures 6-5 and 6-6 using your editor?

4. Design two complex screen displays, one that is easier to store as graphics code and the other that is easier to store as a bit map of the entire screen. What commands are necessary to perform the storage and retrieval of these displays on your system?

5. How important is it that your courseware be transportable to other computer/video systems? How can you optimize transportability of your courseware without sacrificing features?

6. Assume that you have the services of an experienced programmer at your disposal. Plan the development of a CAI course, assigning some of the tasks to yourself and some to your programmer. Put time estimates on each of the tasks. How can you make optimum use of both your skills and those of your programmer?

7. If you will be developing CAI courses that will have to run on a number of different computer/video systems, list the compatible features of these systems. Write programming guidelines to assure that your courseware will run on all of your systems with minimum alterations.

8. What type of auxiliary storage does your computer/video system have: disks, tape, or plug-in memories? Implement the program structure depicted in Figure 6-10 and determine its feasibility using your auxiliary storage device. Is the access time fast enough to make this structure practical?

·7·

CAI Style

Writing in 1973, James Martin stated:

> As yet, no acknowledged sense of style has developed for CAI. . . . In the meantime, however, some singularly unstylish CAI programs are being written.

Martin's use of the term "style" can be interpreted in a number of ways, but certainly one of the main components of style is the tone and feel of the student/computer interaction. This interaction is depicted conceptually in Figure 7-1, which emphasizes that the computer screen is the major channel through which students receive information and is thus the major determinant of the courseware's style.

It is difficult to make a strong case that "stylish" materials teach better than "unstylish" materials, but one study has been done that at least partly supports this hypothesis. Harry McLaughlin (1966) compared the abilities of college undergraduates to locate information in well-produced and poorly produced (verbose) technical pamphlets. He found no significant difference in test performance when the two types of pamphlets were used by *motivated* students. Unmotivated students, however, showed significantly poorer performance when they used the poorly produced pamphlet as compared to their performance with the well-produced one. (This result is consistent with readability studies that show that poorly written materials affect the reading comprehension of poor readers much more than they do that of good readers.) Mc-

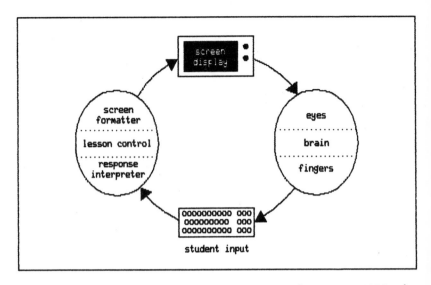

FIGURE 7-1. *The Student/Computer Interaction. (After Heines, 1975, after Schramm, 1954.)*

Laughlin further reported that both motivated and unmotivated students spontaneously stated that *they would not have read the poorer version voluntarily.* He therefore concluded:

> Objective measurement may show that the style of presentation of printed technical matter has little effect upon the efficiency with which information can be culled from it. Yet subjective preferences may be so strong as to make readers ignore material presented in a certain style.

Style is probably the main reason why few people who have interacted personally with a computer have lukewarm feelings about the experience. Most often, people find the interaction either highly enjoyable or totally distasteful (Martin, 1973, and Melnyk, 1972). The strengths of these reactions are an important consideration in the design of CAI programs, as students who find the interaction distasteful will be reluctant to use the computer repeatedly.

Development Guidelines

Most of the distasteful qualities of interactive computer programs may be attributed directly to poor design and poor communication style. The preceding chapters have taken a comprehensive look at screen design styles. The following paragraphs extend those concepts by providing more general guidelines for developing effective student/computer interactions.

Maximize Interaction

Developers sometimes get so hung up on screen design that they lose sight of their original instructional objectives. This preoccupation is often caused by the desire to produce "elegant" screen designs and computer graphics that will be appreciated by the developer's peers. Unfortunately, this elegance is seldom perceived by students who have little or no knowledge of what it takes to put a CAI course together. In the worst case, as previously mentioned, excessive use of visual techniques can actually detract from a program's teaching quality by causing students to "sit back and watch the blinking lights" when they should be concentrating on the subject matter.

Quality screen design and graphics programming take a lot of time. It is therefore understandable that developers might equate the effort needed to implement their designs with the effort needed to implement quality instructional sequences. At its best, however, the use of sophisticated graphics in CAI programs is simply a highly effective way of *presenting* material, for it is basically a *one-way* communication. Quality instructional sequences require *two-way* communication, where students are responding or posing questions to the computer as often as the computer questions or responds to them.

CAI programs should therefore exhibit as much interaction as possible. Students should be drawn into the subject matter rather than be passive viewers watching visual sequences unfold on their screens. The balance between presenting and questioning is crucial, because the higher the level of interaction, the more accurately the program can adapt to individual student differences. (Such adaptions might include providing further details for fast students and additional, reinforcing examples for slower students.) High levels of interaction also decrease student anxiety (Yntema, 1969), yielding a more communicative CAI style and more satisfying student/computer interactions.

Tie Programs In with Other Media

Two other common CAI style problems involve trying to put everything on the computer and trying to put too much information on the screen at one time. The discussion of resolution in Chapter 1, The Computer/Video Medium, should have convinced you that computer screens are not the best vehicles for getting some types of information across. There is no reason why everything you want students to look at has to be displayed on the screen. As an alternative, you might produce a written Student Guide to accompany a CAI program. This guide could include diagrams, photographs, and long text passages that do not lend themselves to computer display. For example, if you want students to read an essay and then use the computer to evaluate what they have read, it will probably be much easier for them to read it off-line than to read it from the screen.

Audio tape is an excellent medium for introducing computer-naive students to CAI, especially when a number of rote tasks must be accomplished to bring up the CAI system. I have used this technique with a CAI program on a large time-sharing system requiring a complex "logon" procedure (Heines, 1974).[1] The use of audio tape proved to be very successful, as all 36 students who used the system were able to get the system up and running without help from an instructor, and none of these students had ever used the system before. The complexity of the logon process is illustrated by the steps listed below:

1. Turn on the terminal.
2. Pick up the phone on the telephone modem.
3. Press the TALK button on the modem.
4. Dial "5."
5. Listen for a high-pitched tone. (This was the signal from the main computer that it was ready to connect to the terminal.)
6. Press the DATA button on the modem so that it lights up.
7. Hang up the phone.
8. Press the RETURN key on the terminal. The computer should respond by typing:

1. "Logging on" is a procedure for gaining access to a large computer that supports several users simultaneously. It usually involves identifying yourself by typing your name or account number followed by a password.

CAPS online   1jh359   gsyosu

9. Press the ATTN key on the terminal. The computer should respond by printing a carriage return and line feed.
10. Type:
    LOGON EDC140 STUDENT

    and press the RETURN key. ("EDC140" was the course identifier, and "student" was the account password.) The computer should respond by typing:
    LOGON AT 10:53:50 DST MONDAY 01/21/74
    U OF ME V1.12 12/22/73
11. Press the RETURN key once again. (This caused the computer to run the CAI program, and all further directions were printed by the program.)

Each of these tasks is simple when considered individually. For computer-naive (and perhaps "computer-phobic") students, however, the process as a whole is quite formidable and the directions are shrouded in "computerese." To overcome this barrier, these instructions were recorded on an audio tape that resided beside the terminal. Students merely had to turn it on to be led through the logon process and hear an overview of how to use the computer.

The use of audio tape for this type of instruction proved to be an excellent choice. Its main advantage was that it freed students from having to read and perform another active task at the same time. Reading itself is an active task and would have necessitated a constant change of visual focus from the written page to the keyboard or computer output and back again. Listening, however, is a more passive task and allowed students to maintain visual focus on the keyboard or computer output without losing touch with the instruction. The effect was similar to having an expert at hand telling students just what to do and pointing out salient aspects of the system while they performed the required actions. While the example shown here is from a large time-sharing system, the use of audio tape is equally adaptable to CAI delivered via microcomputers where students must power the system up, insert one or two diskettes in the proper orientation in the proper disk drives, and then press one or more keys to start the system.

The CAI program discussed above also used 35mm slides as an integral part of the courseware. Most of these slides showed laboratory measuring devices such as stop watches, beam balances, and graduated cylinders that students were asked to read (see Figure 7-2). The fine

FIGURE 7-2. *Setup for Combining 35mm Slides With a CAI Program.*

gradations on the scales of these devices would have been very hard to reproduce realistically on the computer system being used. The slide projector was located next to the terminal, but it was not computer-controlled. The CAI program directed students to view specific slides as illustrations, referring to the slides by their numbered positions in the slide tray and numbers that were printed on the slides themselves. Operation of the projector did not prove to be a problem for the students, and the computer/slide synthesis yielded a highly successful combination of media for teaching the visual skills needed to read laboratory measurements.

The use of complementary media in this manner is a highly effective technique for dealing with the shortcomings of the computer/video medium. If the learning process can be enhanced by directing students to read a passage in a book, study a photograph, or view a film, so be it. Make the book, photograph, or film convenient for students to use, have the program direct them to do the activity off-line, and provide a way for them to indicate to the computer that they have completed the activity so they can continue from where they left off. Do not restrict yourself to a single medium.

Consider Your Student Population

Inability to deal with individual student differences has long been recognized as a major flaw in mass education. As far back as 1906, Edward L. Thorndike cautioned against the wholesale adoption of any specific teaching technique with the following words:

> The practical consequence of the fact of individual differences is that every general law of teaching has to be applied with consideration of the particular person in question.

Individual differences can be dealt with on a number of levels, none of which is particularly easy. At the lowest level, you might at least let students choose their own paths through the courseware via routing menus as discussed in Chapter 4. At the highest level, you might attempt to categorize students by the extent of their prior knowledge, or by their learning styles, and provide different treatments of the subject matter tailored to these individual differences. These multiple treatments usually require far more effort than most developers can give, but are worth mentioning to show the extent of individualization that CAI can achieve.

On a more practical level, sensitivity to the characteristics of your student population can lead to much more concrete guidelines. As stated in Chapter 3, for example, considerations of your student population will probably lead you to avoid cuteness and wisecracks at virtually all costs, especially in testing and problem-solving situations. Cuteness is very difficult to achieve without insulting some members of your student population, especially if you are teaching adults. If students feel that a CAI program is written for people below their level, they will be reluctant to apply themselves to the subject matter.

A smart-aleck style can cause serious damage to the student/computer relationship. A wisecrack that you mean as a joke may hit a student at precisely the wrong time. The last thing one needs when groping with a difficult problem—or a bug in a CAI program—is a smart-aleck, wisecracking computer. Anyone who has had such an experience will probably also testify to having had an overwhelming desire at the time to kick the computer. At their best, wisecracks invariably break students' concentration and detract from the focus on subject matter. At their worst, smart aleck responses may cause students to abandon the CAI program right then and there.

You must be careful to separate your own personal *presentation* style from the style in which you write CAI programs. While you might lean toward a light, jovial, open style when standing before a class, this is difficult to translate to the computer medium. Consider, for example, the differences between what you might *say* in a certain situation and what you might *write* in that same situation. When you are standing in front of a group you can sense students' moods and levels of comprehension and adjust your presentation style accordingly. Unfortunately, computer programs are not quite so flexible. It is therefore best to stick to a rather conservative CAI style, giving the computer a somewhat innocuous personality rather than trying to mimic your own.

Perform Developmental Tests

Developmental tests were mentioned in Chapters 3 and 5 as a method for evaluating the clarity of text messages, and they are relatively easy to perform. You need a working version of your courseware, a number of students who are representative of your target student population, and a room in which you can observe the students as they go through the materials without interruption.

To perform the test, ask your students to ignore you and work through the materials as if you weren't there. Observe their actions and watch their faces for any sign of confusion. Take careful notes on where each student has problems, but do not offer assistance. Even if a student asks for your help, try to refer him or her back to the course materials without providing any additional input unless you feel that the student is really stuck and can't go on. (The biggest problem is avoiding the tendency to help out "just a little.") Let students proceed for a while even if they start going down an incorrect path, just to see if your materials are good enough (provide enough feedback and prompts) to lead them back on track.

After the test is complete, interview the students and try to get them to verbalize where they had problems. If you have trouble picking up students' confusion signs as they work through your material, try letting two students work through the courseware together. This is an excellent technique for achieving verbalization, because the students usually talk to each other and try to achieve consensus before taking any strong actions. Listening to their conversation will let you trace their thinking processes and provide insight into just where they were led astray.

Unfortunately, good developmental testing requires a very precious commodity if its results are to be useful: *time*. Time is needed to perform the tests without rushing students through the courseware, and time is needed to modify the courseware once the tests are completed.

Making revisory decisions based on results of poorly conducted developmental tests is probably more dangerous than not making those revisions at all. If test students are not truly representative of the target population, if they are rushed through the courseware, or if an insufficient number of students are tested, the developmental test data can be badly contaminated. Decisions based on such data will often make a course choppy and destroy its flow. So while it is not necessary for every test student to go through every lesson, it is necessary to have a sufficient number of students go through each lesson. A "sufficient number" in this case is usually at least three students who are representative of the target population but who possess significantly different skill levels. If the students are very homogeneous, a larger number will probably be needed to test the courseware's ability to handle a wider variety of problems.

One nice thing about performing developmental tests is that you can conduct as many as you have time for, concentrating on the weak parts of the course after all parts have been tested. That is, suppose you develop a course consisting of ten lessons and you run six students through five lessons each. Every lesson will then have been tested. You find from these tests that all of the lessons except 2, 7, and 8 perform to your satisfaction with minor changes. These three lessons, however, require some rather basic changes. You can now focus your energies on these changes and conduct new developmental tests on your revised lessons. You might ask all six students to do just these three lessons a second time. The data from this second round of developmental tests should show significant improvement over the first round.

Of course, all the developmental testing in the world will be useless unless your courseware is written in such a way that it can be revised and enough time is allowed to do the revision. Techniques such as the separation of display and lesson logic discussed in Chapter 6 and code documentation can greatly simplify the revision task. These techniques are standard programming practices, and all the rules of good programming apply to CAI as well as to any other program. If you do your own programming, you will want to document your work so you can return to it after a considerable absence. If you cannot include comments throughout the program due to lack of disk space, memory, or language features, create a separate document that describes how the code works, what functions it calls, what data it reads from files, and the meanings of all important variables. If you employ the services of a programmer, insist that the person provide you with this documentation so you can work with another programmer if the first leaves the project.

Final Points

A couple of final guidelines are in order.

Don't Give In to the Machine

The Russians have a particularly terse way of responding to inconvenient requests: they say "Nel-zyah," which means, "It can't be done." It often seems that computer programmers apply this psychology to everyone else's programming requests except their own. A curt, negative reply to a programming request should therefore always be interpreted as,

"Your request is not easy," rather than, "The computer can't do that." Time and again, programmers have proven that there is considerable truth in the saying, "The impossible we do immediately; miracles take a little longer."

There are, of course, some things that computers can't do, but most of the functions that educators want to see in their courseware do not fall into that category. The important point is that you must let your instructional objectives, course content, and lesson strategy drive the programming effort, rather than let the difficulty of programming adversely influence your course design. It is always easier to back off on a difficult design request during a project's implementation phase than to improve a deficient design with a fancy programming trick.

Design your courseware using the most educationally sound and creative techniques at your disposal. Then recruit a programmer, if necessary, to help you implement your design. If trade-offs must be made, a good design will let you assess their impact realistically. With a poor design, however, it will be difficult, if not impossible, to set priorities for the course features on which you are willing to compromise.

Rules Were Meant To Be Broken

Finally, I recommend that you *do not* try to follow all of the guidelines presented in this book. These guidelines reflect my own experience and style, and some may not be suitable for your student population. It has also been impossible to include more than a small number of the possible variations on the specific screen designs shown in this book.

I recommend that you look at as many CAI programs as possible to see additional techniques and gain a fuller understanding of the computer/video medium's capabilities. You will then be in an excellent position to begin developing your own CAI style by becoming intimately familiar with your own system's capabilities, experimenting with various screen design techniques, and assessing through developmental testing which of these are most appropriate for your students.

Chapter Summary

The style of student/computer interactions is an important factor in determining how students view CAI programs and whether they will find the experience of taking a CAI course enjoyable. Given the role of the computer screen as the major channel through which students view the computer, it is reasonable to conclude that screen design is one of the major determinants in establishing a program's style.

A number of other guidelines can also contribute to effective CAI style:

• Maximize interaction.

• Tie programs in with other media.

• Consider the experience of your target student population.

• Perform developmental tests, basing courseware revisions on their results.

These guidelines are all supplemental to the screen design techniques discussed in previous chapters and should be used to complement those techniques when planning your courseware at the highest level.

Instructional quality, rather than programming difficulty, should be the driving force in courseware design. While programming considerations should be kept in mind at all stages, it is better to compromise on programming requests during the implementation phase than to handicap yourself by worrying excessively about programming during the design phase.

The guidelines presented in this book reflect my own experience and style and should be tailored to meet the specific needs of your student population. You should try to develop your own CAI style by becoming intimately familiar with your own system's capabilities, experimenting with various screen design techniques, and assessing through developmental testing which of these are most appropriate for your students.

Issues and Activities

1. What possibilities exist for tying your CAI programs in with other media? Would slides or movies be useful adjuncts to your courseware? How might you set up such equipment so students can use it as they work through CAI materials?

2. Conduct a number of developmental tests on a CAI program. (The program need not be original; use any program to which you have access.) Are there points in the program where students stumble consistently? How might you correct the program's deficiencies using the data collected during your test?

3. Make an audio tape like that described in this chapter to get students up and running one of your CAI programs. Try out the tape in a number of developmental tests to evaluate its effectiveness.

4. Analyze a number of CAI programs to assess their level of interaction. Do the programs make you feel involved with the subject matter or are they predominantly computerized slide shows?

5. Analyze a number of CAI programs to assess their abilities to adapt to individual differences. Do the programs offer a large number of alternate paths through the material, or do all students go through the program along virtually the same path?

6. Analyze a number of CAI programs to assess the effectiveness of their presentation styles. Are they friendly and helpful or wisecracking and abrasive? Do you think that these programs' styles are appropriate for the students they are intended to teach?

7. Assume that you will be developing courseware in a team environment. Write a short list of screen formatting standards that can be used by the team to assure that all materials have a consistent look and feel. Where should orientation information go, and with what text attributes should it be displayed? What types of menus will you use for routing and student options? What conventions should the entire team adhere to for both text and graphics?

8. What are the major features of your target student population that you should consider in designing CAI materials? Are they good or poor readers? Are they computer-naive or computer-literate? Are they familiar with keyboards or will they find typing difficult? Will they relate better to text or to graphics displays? How can you tailor your courseware to your students' unique characteristics?

Glossary

Aliasing. See *staircasing*.

Animation. Repetitive positioning of the cursor and displaying of a symbol to make the symbol appear to move across the screen. The cursor is typically repositioned one or more spaces or pixels to the right, left, up, or down before each successive display.

Anti-aliasing. One of a variety of techniques for reducing *staircasing*.

ASCII. Abbreviation for "American Standard Code for Information Interchange." The term ASCII is also used on its own to refer to the ASCII standard character set. This character set defines the characters that will be printed when each of 128 standard bit sequences are sent to a terminal. For example, ASCII character number 65 (decimal) is a capital letter "A", and ASCII character number 97 is a lowercase "a". ASCII character number 7 rings the terminal's bell (or sounds its buzzer).

Attribute. An optional characteristic of a graphic entity such as color, flashing, bolding, reverse video, etc. that changes the appearance of that entity but does not change its basic nature or position on the screen.

Bit map. The internal method by which computers represent a screen's dot matrix. The size of the bit map is a factor in determining the resolution of the screen and depends on the amount of the computer's memory dedicated to this purpose. The bit map contains one or more bits for each point on the screen and contains information about whether that point is on or off, what color it is, etc.

Bit-mapped screen. A screen that is represented by a bit map.

Blinking. The intermittent display of a graphic entity. (Synonym for *flashing*.)

Boldface. A type font in which the main strokes of the letter are thicker than normal.

CAI.   Abbreviation for *computer-assisted* (or *computer-aided*) *instruction.*

Callable.   In the sense used in this book, *callable* refers to the ability of graphics code to be accessed from within a CAI program. This means that callable code (usually to draw graphics on the screen) can be stored on disk and then called into action when needed rather than being part of the CAI program wirtten in some computer language.

Carriage return.   The act of moving the screen writing position (usually indicated by a *cursor*) to the left-hand margin. This action is commonly initiated by printing ASCII character number 13 (decimal). The term is borrowed from typewriter terminology where pushing the carriage lever (on manual typewriters) or pressing the RETURN key (on electric typewriters) positions the carriage so that the next character typed will appear at the left-hand margin. Note that typewriters (and many computer terminals) actually perform a *carriage return/line feed pair* when the carriage lever is pushed or the RETURN key is pressed. (Compare with *carriage return/line feed pair, line feed,* and *line terminator.*)

Carriage return/line feed pair.   The act of moving the screen writing position (usually indicated by a *cursor*) to the left-hand margin of the next lower line. This action is usually the combination of two subactions, *carriage return* and *line feed,* and is commonly initiated by printing ASCII character numbers 13 and 10 (decimal).

Cathode ray tube (CRT).   A television-like screen that displays information generated by a computer program.

CBI.   Abbreviation for *computer-based instruction.*

Character cell.   A small rectangular dot matrix that is used to display a single character. Characters cells are typically found in sizes of 5x7, 7x9, 8x16, or 10x20 dots (horizontal by vertical).

Character cell level system.   A system that is only capable of addressing entire character cells, not individual dots on the screen.

Character set.   The full collection of patterns with which a system can fill a character cell by printing a single character on the screen.

Character set editor.   A program to simplify the creation and modification of author-defined character sets by converting patterns drawn on the screen to the 1s and 0s needed to specify the character's bit map to the computer.

CMI.   Abbreviation for *computer-managed instruction.*

Computer-assisted (or **computer-aided) instruction (CAI).**   The use of a computer system as a tutor. The computer presents instruction to students using text and graphics to illustrate important points and allows students to interact with the computer to practice the skills being taught.

Computer-based instruction (CBI).   The entire field of using interactive computers to enhance instruction, including both CAI and CMI.

Computer-managed instruction (CMI).   The use of a computer system to control and/or monitor students' paths through instructional material. Many CMI systems have CAI components, but this is not true on all systems. The computer's main function in CMI is to store data on student performance and prescribe future instruction based on this data.

Creeping.   A type of scrolling in which text moves horizontally across the screen like a news wire moving along the bottom of a television program. Other examples of creeping include news flashes on the Allied Chemical Building in New York City's Times Square and the wall-type Dow Jones ticker displayed in many large brokerage firms.

CRT.   Abbreviation for *cathode ray tube.*

Cursor.   An indicator on a computer screen that indicates where the next character typed by the user or printed by the computer will be displayed.

Descenders.   Those parts of a letter that "go below the line" on which the letter is written. Descenders are found on the lowercase letters g, j, p, q, and y.

Developmental testing.   A process for evaluating instructional materials in which students are observed as they work. This process tests many of the materials' basic qualities and should be made early enough in the course development cycle to allow for extensive revisions.

Display logic.   The code needed to generate displays on a computer screen. Display logic may include computer language statements, special character sequences to be printed in graphics mode, and/or algorithms needed to generate graphic displays. (Compare with *lesson logic.*)

Dot matrix.   A rectangular array of dots. Each dot may be either on or off and possibly possess a number of graphic attributes such as color, flashing, bolding, etc. The dot represents the smallest addressable point on the screen.

Echo.   The act of printing on the screen characters that are typed by students. This is the normal mode of operation; but in some instances, such as typing code names and passwords that should remain secret, echoing of typed characters can be turned off.

Filling.   Making a graphic area solid by turning on all the dots within its boundary. Filling may be implemented in either hardware or software, but is usually accessible through one or two simple graphic commands if it is available at all.

Fill line.   A line that indicates one boundary of an area to be filled. Designers typically specify a fill line before drawing a more complex figure such as a curve or irregular polygon. As the more complex figure is being drawn, the system automatically draws lines to fill in all the points between the figure and the full line. Fill lines are sometimes difficult to use with complex and/or obliquely positioned figures, but the process of filling to a line is often much faster than filling to a point (see *fill point*).

Fill point. A point that indicates the radial center of an area to be filled. Designers typically specify a fill point before surrounding it with a more complex figure such as a curve or irregular polygon. As the more complex figure is being drawn, the system automatically draws lines from the figure to the fill point to fill in the entire area. Fill points are sometimes conceptually easier to use than fill lines, but the process of filling to a point is often much slower than filling to a line (see *fill line*).

Flashing. The intermittent display of a graphic entity. (Synonym for *blinking*.)

Font. A type style that is distinctive in some *basic* way from other type styles. Fonts differ from each other in more than just attributes (see the definition of *attributes* above). They differ in the way characters are shaped and the "feel" that the text connotes.

Function keys. Special keyboard keys that perform specified functions rather than displaying characters on the screen. For example, students can use function keys on the PLATO system to get help and back up the instruction to the previous display.

Graphics mode. A state of the video part of a computer/video system in which characters received from the computer part represent graphics commands or special characters to be displayed on the screen rather than in standard text.

Informational television. A style of television presentation whose main purpose is to convey information to the viewer rather than to entertain. Examples of informational television include news programs, documentaries, and certain educational productions for children.

Inverse video. See *reverse video.*

Italicization. The slanting of a character cell so that the basic shape of the cell is distorted from a rectangle to a parallelogram. (Compare with *letter rotation* and *writing line rotation.*)

Justification. The alignment of text margins. *Left-justified* text has a straight left margin, while *right-justified* text has a straight right margin. Text with both margins straight is often referred to simply as "justified." (The opposite of justified is *ragged.*)

Kerning. The overlapping of letter combinations such as "AV" and "LY" in typeset text so that the apparent interletter distances remain the same as those between other pairs of letters in the typeface.

Keyword.   In a menu, a single word that serves as an abbreviation for one of the options.

Lesson.   As used in this text, a subunit of a course module that usually addresses only one or two instructional objectives. (Compare with *module*.)

Lesson logic.   The code needed to control lesson flow in a CAI program. Lesson logic typically takes the form of a computer program and does *not* include the commands necessary to generate screen displays. (Compare with *display logic*.)

Letter rotation.   Rotation of an entire character cell without distorting the basic rectangular shape of the cell. (Compare with *italicization* and *writing line rotation*.)

Line feed.   The act of moving the screen writing position (usually indicated by a *cursor*) straight down to the next lower line. This action is commonly initiated by printing ASCII character number 10 (decimal). The term is borrowed from electric typewriter terminology where pressing the LINE FEED key (sometimes also called the INDEX key) advances the paper one line. (Compare with *carriage return, carriage return/line feed pair*, and *line terminator*.)

Line terminator.   A character or set of characters that marks the end of a line. The most common line terminator is a *carriage return/line feed pair*.

Menu.   A screen display designed to present students with a number of fixed options and allow them to choose the option they desire.

Module.   As used in this text, a unit of a course that usually addresses a small set of related instructional objectives. (Compare with *lesson*.)

Monochromatic.   Made up of a single primary color (red, green, or blue).

Mouse.   An auxiliary computer input device for indicating screen positions. The mouse is actually a small box that can be rolled on a flat surface. The length and direction of its movement is monitored by the computer to determine the corresponding screen position.

Pixel.   The smallest addressable point on a video screen. (Abbreviation for *picture element*.)

Pixel multiplier.   A technique for enlarging bit-mapped characters in which the number of dots turned on by each 1 bit in the character bit map is basically two for Size 2 characters, three for Size 3 characters, and so on.

PLATO.   A large CBI system, marketed by Control Data Corporation, that was developed at the University of Illinois under the direction of Donald Bitzer in the late 1960s and early 1970s. The major features of this system are: (1) it uses a very large Cyber mainframe computer (a Control Data product) to drive the system and is therefore very expensive (several million dollars to purchase) but can support a very large number of simultaneous users (1–2 thousand); (2) the system uses an 8½ inch square display screen consisting of a 512x512 dot matrix which is capable of excellent graphic renditions and was also one of the first such graphic displays in wide use in an educational environment; (3) more courseware has been developed for this system than for any other existing system; (4) all existing PLATO systems in the U.S. (about twelve) are tied together in a large network and can share courseware and other communications with each other. PLATO is an acronym for "Programmed Learning for Automatic Teaching Operations." (Compare with *TICCIT.*)

Pop erase.   A method for erasing graphic entities that clears parts of the screen in a single action, so that all dots appear to turn off simultaneously. (Compare with *wipe erase.*)

Prerequisite.   An instructional unit whose objectives must be mastered before students are allowed to study the module in question. That is, if Module 5 has both Modules 3 and 4 as prerequisites, both of these modules must be completed before the student studies Module 5.

Primitive.   An action that can be performed easily by a system. For example, "erase from cursor to end of line" is usually a primitive in most CAI systems, but "erase block" is not. The "erase block" function must be broken down into a series of primitives that the system can execute.

Program.   As a noun, a set of instructions that direct a computer to perform some meaningful task. Such instructions are written in computer languages such as BASIC, Fortran, Tutor, etc. As a verb, the act of writing such instructions and storing them on a computer system.

Ragged.   Not justified. (See *justification.*)

Raster.   As used in this book, synonym for *dot matrix.*

Raster scan systems.   Computer/video systems that display text and pictures using a dot matrix. (Compare with *stroke vector systems.*)

Resolution.   A characteristic of picture quality determined by the size of the dots that make up the picture. The smaller the dots and the shorter the distance between adjacent dots, the "finer" the resolution. (Synonyms for "finer" here include "greater," "higher," and "better.")

Reverse video.   A graphic technique in which entities are displayed as dark lines or points on a light background. In terms of bit maps, reverse video is achieved by turning on all dots corresponding to 0s and turning off all dots corresponding to 1s, as opposed to normal video which turns on all dots corresponding to 1s and turning off all dots corresponding to 0s. (Reverse video is referred to as *inverse video* on some systems.)

Router. A program to move students from one instructional unit to another, such as between modules or between lessons.

Routing menu. A menu that allows students to choose the instructional unit that they will study next.

Scrolling. Moving an entire area of the screen simultaneously. The most common cause of scrolling is a carriage return/line feed pair printed when the cursor is positioned on the last line of the screen. In this case, the entire screen image moves upward to make room for another line of text at the bottom of the screen. The text or graphics that were previously at the top of the screen are said to "scroll off the screen," are lost permanently, and cannot be retrieved. Some systems, most notably the PLATO system, do not scroll at all. When a carriage return/line feed pair is printed with the cursor positioned on the last line of these systems, the cursor most often moves to the beginning of the top line of the screen without erasing anything.

Scrolling area or **scrolling region.** An area on the screen in which scrolling takes place. Scrolling areas can be restricted (usually between two horizontal lines) so that printing a carriage return/line feed pair with the cursor positioned on the last line of the scrolling area causes only the text and graphics within the defined area to scroll. The top line of the scrolling area is lost permanently and cannot be retrieved, but any text or graphic outside the scrolling area is not affected.

Serifs. Fine lines that finish off the ends of the main strokes of a letter.

Staircasing. A characteristic of lines drawn on dot matrix screens that makes them appear jagged rather than smooth. The degree of staircasing depends on the angle at which the line is drawn (horizontal and vertical lines do not exhibit staircasing) and the resolution of the screen. Finer screens exhibit far less staircasing than coarse ones. All dot matrix screens, however, exhibit some degree of staircasing, although very expensive graphics systems have a number of techniques to minimize the undesirable effects of this phenomenon. (Synonym of *aliasing*.)

Stroke vector systems. Computer/video systems that employ oscilloscope-like technology to achieve direct control of the electron beam that draws on the screen. Stroke vector systems are an alternate technology to *raster scan systems*. Their main advantage is that they exhibit very high resolution with no staircasing, but they are generally much more expensive than raster scan systems. (Compare with *raster scan systems*.)

Symbol. A visual entity that carries some specific meaning to students.

TICCIT. A large CBI system, marketed by the Mitre Corporation, that was developed at Brigham Young University under the direction of C.

Victor Bunderson in the late 1960s and early 1970s. The major features of this system are: (1) it uses two couple processors to drive the system and is relatively expensive (about $500,000 to purchase) but can support 128 simultaneous users; (2) the system displays its output on color TV screens and was one of the first instructional systems to use color TV coupled to a computer system; (3) the system has not enjoyed very wide use, but the courseware developed for it is of above average quality due to intrinsic human-engineering features in the system software. TICCIT is an acronym for "Time-shared Interactive Computer-Controlled Instructional Television." (Compare with *PLATO*.)

Time-sharing systems.   Large computer systems that can be used by many students simultaneously while appearing to be dedicated to each individual user.

Transportability.   The ease with which a program that runs on one system can be made to run on another system of a different type.

Tree structure.   As used in this text, a way to structure menus such that each option on a higher level menu branches to a separate menu at a lower level. An example of a tree structure might have module names at the highest level. Selecting a module causes branching to a lower level menu that lists the names of each component lesson in that particular module.

Type style.   The basic "look" of a body of text determined by the way in which its characters are formed.

VDU.   Abbreviation for *video display unit*.

Video display unit.   A television-like screen used to display output from a computer system.

Wipe erase.   A method for erasing graphic entities that clears parts of the screen in a sweeping action. Wipe erases resemble the action of passing an eraser over a chalkboard. Two important characteristics of wipe erases are that they proceed slowly and have a definite directional quality. These characteristics require designers to be sensitive to the way students' eyes are guided as the erasure proceeds. (Compare with *pop erase*.)

Writing line rotation.   A change in the direction of the base line on which text is written. (Compare with *letter rotation* and *italicization*.)

Bibliography

BORK, Alfred 1981. *Learning with Computers*. Bedford, MA: Digital Press.

BORK, Alfred 1982. "Information Display and Screen Design." Paper presented at a conference of the American Education Research Association, 1982, New York.

BRAUN, L.; Laio, T.; Pressel, D.; Lasik, C.; Williamson, E.; and Yourda, M. 1971. *POLUT Resource Handbook*. Huntington Two Computer Project. Polytechnic Institute of Brooklyn, NY.

CONTROL DATA CORPORATION 1979. *Control Data PLATO CMI System Overview*. Minneapolis: Control Data Corporation.

GREGORY, Margaret and Poulton, E.C. 1970. "Even Versus Uneven Right-Hand Margins and the Rate of Comprehension in Reading." *Ergonomics* 13(4): 427–434.

HEINES, Jesse M. 1974. "An Interactive, Computer-Managed Model for the Evaluation of Audio-Tutorial Instruction." Unpublished Master's Thesis, University of Maine at Orono.

HEINES, Jesse M. 1975. "Style and Communication in Interactive Programming." In *Proceedings of the 1975 Conference of the Association for the Development of Computer-based Instructional Systems*. Bellingham, VA: Association for the Development of Computer-based Instructional Systems.

HOFSTETTER, Fred 1975. "GUIDO: An Interactive Computer-Based System for Improvement of Instruction and Research in Ear Training." *Journal of Computer-based Instruction* 1:100–106.

HYATT, Gary W.; Eades, David C.; and Tenczar, Paul 1972. "Computer-Based Education in Biology." *BioScience* 22(7):401–409.

MARTIN, James 1973. *Design of Man-Computer Dialogues*. Englewood Cliffs, NJ: Prentice-Hall, Inc.

McLAUGHLIN, G. Harry 1966. "Comparing Styles of Presenting Technical Information." *Ergonomics* 9(3):257–259.

MELNYK, Vera 1972. "Man-Machine Interface: Frustration." *Journal of the American Society for Information Science* 23(6):392–401.

MOREAU, Ken and Heines, Jesse M. 1975. "Creating Graphic Displays on Non-Graphics Terminals." In *Proceedings of the 1975 Conference of the Association for the Development of Computer-based Instructional Systems*. Bellingham, VA: Association for the Development of Computer-based Instructional Systems.

SANDBURG, Carl 1954. *Abraham Lincoln*. New York: Dell Publishing Co., Inc.

SCHRAMM, Wilbur, ed. 1954. "How Communication Works." *The Process and Effects of Mass Communication*, pp. 3–10. Urbana, IL: University of Illinois Press.

SEILER, Bonnie Anderson and Weaver, Charles S. 1974. *Description of PLATO Whole Number Arithmetic Games*. Champaign, IL: Computer Based Education Research Laboratory, The University of Illinois.

THORNDIKE, Edward L. 1906. *The Principles of Teaching*. New York: The MacMillan Company.

YNTEMA, D.B. 1969. "Engineering Psychology in Man-Computer Interaction." Paper presented at the 1969 Annual Convention of the American Psychological Association, San Francisco.

Index